This book is dedicated to my Father John "Johnny" Langan.

Johnny was born during the Depression in the Bronx to Irish immigrants. They lived in an overcrowded two bedroom walk up with five other family members. He was the first in our family to attend College. He graduated from St. Francis College in Pennsylvania. He went on to attend St John's Law School where he met my Mother Adrienne. He always said when he retired he would write a book about his experiences practicing law for over 40 years. He never got around to it and passed in 2016 at the age of 83. Hope you love the book Dad.

I'll see you on the other side….

Introduction

This book started out as a reflection of attending six Super Bowls. To inform people how to acquire tickets and figure out the logistics of securing transportation and lodging. The title comes from the players, it's slang for making it to the Super Bowl! This Summer I decided to finally write it. As I put pen to paper, it became much more than that. This book spans Five decades. It's the condensed version of 49 years of my life as it pertains to my experiences with Football. It reveals how this great sport parallels life. The incredible bonds you form being a player to becoming a fan. The journey that spans generations from Father & Son to Brothers & Friends and back to where it all started. I attended my first Football game with my Father as a rite of passage. I attended my first Super Bowl with my brother and the last with my son. Along the way, I have learned many lessons. I hope you enjoy reading this book as much as I have loved living it. Some of the names have been changed but the stories are true with a little embellishment. Lately, Football has been shown in a bad light with the kneeling controversy and the CTE discovery. I admire the leagues for taking action. The improved equipment and rule changes will hopefully keep the players safer. The book focuses on all the positive aspects of the sport and the joy it brings to its participants and fans.

Table of Contents

Chapter One The Curse Begins

I was born in Brooklyn, New York in 1961.We moved to Staten Island before they built the Verrazano Narrows Bridge which spanned the Hudson River. The only way to get there from Manhattan or Brooklyn was by ferry. Staten Island was the 5th and forgotten borough of NYC. Manhattan and Brooklyn were the most prominent followed by the Bronx which hosted the NY Yankees and NY Giants for a while. Queens came next where the NY Mets Baseball team shared Shea Stadium with the NY Jets Football team. The Middle Class or Blue-collar borough of Staten Island was under developed at that time. We had one train, two ferry's and three bridges that connected us to New Jersey. Geographically, we might as well be in New Jersey.

It was a cool Fall day in 1970, when 20 kids or so gathered to play football on David St. No one had backyards big enough to play ball in. CAR!!! Car!!! Similar to an official whistle signaling a timeout. We all moved to the sidewalk to avoid the oncoming traffic. We had to overcome other obstacles as well.

The lower hanging branches of the large Sycamore trees and the telephone wires made passing extremely difficult. It was suburban street ball. Go to the manhole and button hook. Run behind the Blue Chrysler and wait for my toss. “Quintessential Street Ball”. If you fell down, you got cut and you bled as the pavement was unforgiving.

Everyone wanted to play the Quarterback position. They wanted to be Joe Namath, Joe Willy. The brash young QB out of Alabama who led to NY Jets in an epic underdog win in Super Bowl III against the highly favored Baltimore Colt led by veteran QB Johnny Unitas. With this epic win The Jets were on top of the Sports World! They single handedly brought the much-maligned American football Conference to the front pages where they gained respect. The fan favorite National Football League recognized this, and it forced their hands to merge with the upstart American Football League to form what is the present-day NFL National Football League.

I was 9 years old, I don’t even recall watching the game to be honest with you. You see, the Super Bowl was a relatively new experience. In the beginning, it wasn’t even taken seriously! In 1967, it was first called the AFL-NFL Championship. It wasn’t until the 3rd Game In 1969, the name of the game was coined Super Bowl by Kansas City Chiefs owner Lamar Hunt. The inspiration came from the kids toy Super Ball! They changed it from Superball to Super Bowl. Most kids knew what that was but showed little interest in the actual Super Bowl Game. In fact, neither did most adults. The first Super Bowl they had to give tickets away just to fill the stadium. It was so long ago; Buffalo Chicken Wings didn't even exist.

My father took me to my first professional Football game. Later I realized this is a rite of passage. The game featured the hometown the NY Jets versus the San Diego Chargers in Shea Stadium. We walked into the stadium, I can remember it as if it were yesterday. The stadium lights glared brightly even though it was a day game. The colors were electric as if they glowed in the dark. This was the early days of color television. I believe the colors had to be this vibrant to show up on the TV's at home. We sat in the end zone bleachers and it was extremely cold as the November winds ripped through Shea Stadium. Thank God we had a thermos full of hot cocoa that my mother had packed. We ate soggy pretzels and focused on the teams doing battle in front of us. It was a low scoring game that the Jets won. After the final whistle, the players with their muddy uniforms ran off the field. We scrambled to get autographs by the tunnel which led to the locker rooms but were unsuccessful. On that cold rainy windswept day, I was baptized for the second time. It was official, I was a Jet Fan.

When we had our victory in Super Bowl III, we finally had some bragging rights against the kids who were NY Giants fans. Who knew that the old saying "Be careful what you wish for" would never ring truer. What first turned out to be a Celebration later turned out to be a curse. It's been 49 Years since the JETS appeared in a Super Bowl.

Chapter 1a The Monticello Room

Later that year, we moved into a better neighborhood and into a bigger house. It was a 4bedroom yellow stucco house that sat on an acre of land. It could barely be seen from the street due to the mature trees and shrubbery. There were three towering Sierra Pines that had 4-foot diameter trunks. It had a 50-yard long driveway with a beautiful rock garden and towering Holly trees. We had Apple and Pear trees and a huge vegetable garden. It was as if we had moved to the country. Our family was comprised of four brothers. In the new neighborhood, we continued to play street ball and even had a yard to play tackle in as well.

Before you knew it one by one we entered High School and played ball. It was the mid-seventies we bought our first Color TV and watched the Jets on Sunday. The TV was placed at the southern end of a long narrow room. The dimensions were 7 feet by about 20 feet. There were two couches and a chair. The room had that 1970's wood paneling and a shag carpet. Somehow all six of us fit in there comfortably to watch TV. On game days, friends would also cram into this narrow space to enjoy the games. Keep in mind that my brothers are all over 6 ft tall and over 200 pounds. My younger brother's friends later dubbed this the "Monticello Room" after the street we lived on. Getting a seat in there to watch a special game was coveted. My Mother's incredible Italian cooking just added to the allure.

Football and the NFL became more popular when they added Monday Night Football. The Dallas Cowboys and the Pittsburgh Steelers were now the teams to beat. The Super Bowl became very popular. Fans began throwing parties and office pools and betting became mainstream. The NFL was quickly growing into the most popular sport in the USA.

I remember going to my grandmother's house in Brooklyn and there was this neighbor who would stop by often. His name was Al. I later found out that he was related to one of my Uncles. I remembered him as an average height, middle aged man, balding, with a mustache. He would have a drink in one hand and a cigarette in the other. He always wore high collared shirts with the first 3 buttons opened to show off his gold chains. In between puffs of his Kent cigarette he talked with a quick delivery. A rat-a -tat cadence almost like a fire cracker. Well, one topic led to another and the subject of sports came up. Eventually Football came up between one of my uncles and Al. I was sitting at the kitchen table listening to the banter when I heard Al say that he had been to every Super Bowl all 5!!! I thought that was cool. I never even imagined going to a Super Bowl. At the time, I thought he must be a big fan of the game to spend the time and effort to attend the last and hopefully the best game of the season.

The years slipped by as they always do and now I'm thirteen and I graduated from St Clare's Grammar School and I followed my older brother's choice of High School's. Monsignor Farrell High School was an all-boys private catholic School run by Christian Brothers. We had an excellent Football team. We were ranked number 13 in the nation. I played Linebacker as well as Offensive Guard, mostly second string. In September of 1977 our team charted a jet and we flew to Cincinnati Ohio to play the number one team in the nation, Moeller High School. We had to sell 150 dollars' worth of 10dollar chances to offset the cost. It was my first time on an airplane.

When we disembarked there was a band to meet us as well as the local news channel. It was Big Time! It was written up as the Super Bowl of HS Football. Even Sports Illustrated wrote about the match up. We played at Nippert Stadium in front of 30,000 fans. Sadly, we lost 33-0 after having two of our scores were called back. The excitement was surreal. It was my first experience of Big Time Football. Several of the players on Moeller went on to play in the NFL including Bob Crable who was at least a foot taller than me or so it seemed when I met him.

On the plane ride home, I realized I probably wasn't going to have a career in Football but what an awesome experience. Both College and Professional players get to do this every other week.

A year later, it was off to College and my playing days were behind me. Now Football became a spectator sport and I became one of its biggest fans. After college it was off to Wall street where Sports were even a bigger deal. I worked with one of the NY Giants owner's sons.

Gambling on games became even more evident on the floors of the Stock Exchanges. They bet on everything from a flip of the coin to who would win the NCAA Basketball final Four. In 1985, I recall some desk trader at Solomon Brothers had bet against Georgetown Hoyas and Patrick Ewing. If he lost it would have been in the hundreds of thousands of dollars. It was a tight game, but coach Rollie Massimino and the underdog Villanova Wildcats pulled out the upset.

But the Grand Daddy of them all was a Million Dollar Box Pool $10,000 a box. Way too rich for my blood. I was a floor reporter making $180 dollars a week. I was struggling to try to get hired as a Specialist Clerk at the time. There was a $5000 Dollar Pool ran by this Floor Trader named Hank who also owned two restaurants in the city. I took stamped my # 176 in a box for $50 dollars. All the brokers had stamps representing their Seat or Membership numbers.

Friday was the big day they drew the numbers in the trading pit. All his buddies seemed to get great numbers 3-0, 7-7, 7-3.... After a while I was wondering if it was rigged. I waited my turn to get a copy of the sheets representing the numbers. I asked Clem what does 176 have he said 8-6. Crappy numbers 8-6 there goes my fifty bucks. He looked at me and said why don't you come to my restaurant on the upper East side and watch the game. I said I'll ask my girlfriend and see if we can make it. 8-6 are you kidding me? WTF? Well at least I received an invite. Maybe I can make more connections and move up the ladder career wise. It was 1985.

Super Bowl XIX featured the San Francisco 49ers against the Miami Dolphins. There were 84,059 in attendance. Dan Marino the former Pittsburgh College QB against Joe Montana the former Notre Dame QB. I knew it would be an epic Battle. At least I would be off my parent's couch and in the City at a bar watching the game.

We arrived at the Bar & Restaurant "Wolfies" just prior to kick off. It was January 20th a snowy, blustery day. I found Henry in a booth with his friends and some family members. We ate snacks and had a drink, The Miami Dolphins pulled out to an early lead the 1st quarter ended 10-7 Miami. I'm sure one of his buddies collected the first $500 Bucks, it was a $5000-dollar pool in all. The Breakdown was $500 for the 1st quarter and 1250 for the half, then $750 for the 3rd quarter and $2500 for the final.

We gave the waiter our entrees and watched the second quarter at Half Time the score was 2816 as San Francisco pulled ahead. Henry pulled out the sheet and said the winner was 176. I was too busy talking about trying to get a job to realize I had just won. He called over one of his workers and I was paid $1250. I was in a bit of shock since this was two months' pay plus the fact that I won with 86. My Girlfriend smiled gave me a kiss. I asked if I should tip the worker he said no. So, I went to the bar and ordered a bottle of Dom Perignon for the table, He said thanks and informed me that it was his Birthday. I was on cloud nine.

We all watched the halftime show. By this time the storm had gotten worse and there was 4 inches on the ground and blizzard conditions. The 3rd quarter began, and Miami laid an egg while San Francisco scored 10 points. Now in Box pools you only go by the last digit. So now the score was San Fran 38 Miami 16. So, 8-6 wins again. The worker comes over and hands me another $750 dollars. Now I'm feeling a bit uneasy. I never won that much money in my life. I attempted to be a gracious winner and I bought another bottle of Dom Perignon Champagne and drinks for the dwindling patrons at the bar. I never had any experience being a gracious winner, but I gave it my best shot.

There was an uneasy tension at the table, which seemed to ease as we drank the bubbly. We sang Happy Birthday and he blew out the candles and cut the cake. During dinner conversation I came to find out that his guests included his daughter, his ex-wife, and his present girlfriend. I thought that was a bit odd but was glad to see he had an open mind. Once again, our conversation turned to business. The jobs he was offering were not the ones I cared to follow up on. We ordered coffee and the 4th quarter dragged on as 38-16 was already a blowout. With 3 minutes left I realized no one had scored. Now my eyes were glued to the screen. Every missed pass, every run out of bounds, every time out became more magnified and more crucial. Miami had little or no chance to come back and win. It wasn't mathematically impossible, but it was highly improbable.

Tic, tic, tic every second seemed like an hour.... I repeated the mantra don't score, don't score. don't score. My heart began to beat faster. Ironically, it's the exact opposite of what everyone else watching the game wanted. Apart from the very few of us who had 8-6. Could this be happening? No one was going to score in the 4th QTR of a Super Bowl. Everyone in the BOX POOL Universe knows the Final score is the big payout. Could this be happening. Could this $180 dollar a week floor reporter takes the lion share of a pool where wealthy traders had the numbers with the highest probability of winning? It doesn't seem feasible.

When the final whistle blew I jumped out of my seat. San Francisco 38 Miami 16 !!!! It was the same score once again. I won another $2500 Dollars. The blizzard roared outside but I hit a fever pitch inside. I was ecstatic the worker came over paid me. In a $5000 pool I had won $4500. As far as I know this has never happened before or since, this means the winner of the Million Dollar Pool collected around $875,000.

It was late we said our goodbyes. His ex-wife asked him to escort me out to the parking garage, so I wouldn't get rolled carrying all that cash. He replied: He's a big guy he can take care of himself. I was through being the gracious winner I was celebrating. Growing up in NYC I doubted there were any thieves out in a Blizzard. They usually prey on the weak and this would be too much work on a cold night. I drove my girlfriend home gave her a couple of $100 bills to go shopping. I then set out to make it back to Staten Island as the storm intensified. When I get back home my younger Brother and Mother were still up. I walked into the Monticello room where they were watching TV and threw all the cash up in the air. The room was covered with dead presidents. I spent the next half hour unfolding the incredible events that transpired that night.

Chapter 2 Moving Up The Ladder

It was the mid 80's, I had parlayed my Floor Reporter Job into a Specialists Clerk's Position. Believe it or not I took a $25 a week pay cut to take the job. Sometimes in life you may have to take a step backwards to get ahead in the future. I went to Finance School at night to learn how to trade options and chart Equities. Wall Street was exploding! Firms needed bodies to handle the increased volume of Business. The pace was frantic or frenetic, pick you poison. If you had a sharp mind and quick reflexes this was the place for you. Numbers ran through my head day and night. Symbols, stocks, data, prices all day and night flowing through my head in an endless steam. Computers were just beginning to be utilized. Technology was exploding. Every morning I was up at 5 am. I took a train, then a ferry, then walked a mile just to get to work by 7 am. At 5 PM, I took a train uptown for classes several days a week then back home. Days and nights all blended together. The hard work paid off soon I was able to take the bus which wad $3 dollars compared to the $1 train ride and .25 cent Ferry fare.

Weekends were for Fun, Family & Football. It was time to destress and recharge your battery. My younger brother had become one of the best offensive lineman on the East Coast. He was being heavily recruited. After months of deliberation he signed with Cornell, the same college our older brother had graduated in 1982. The Ivy Leagues don't give out sports scholarships. NY State subsidizes several of the sub-schools at the University making it more affordable.

That Summer, my younger brother became a Ball Boy for the NY Giants. It was the Summer of 1984. I'm 22 years old at this point. I drove up to Giant Camp to meet him. I was able to meet Lawrence Taylor, Jim Burt and some of the other lineman. It was amazing to meet and talk to the players. We watched them practice then headed back home.

The Following year he took a job with Converse Sneakers instead of the NY Giants. It was no loss to me as I was really a die-hard Jet fan either way. Wouldn't you know it the Giants end up going all the way and "GO TO THE SHOW" in Players vernacular. They ended up playing and winning the Super Bowl in Pasadena. They Beat the New England Patriots 17-14. Even the staff received Rings. Perhaps if he was full time he would have earned one. Instead, my brother received 3 pairs of Converse Sneakers that Summer. My brother later went on to win the Ivy League Championship and earned a Championship Ring of his own. It's Funny how life works out sometimes.

It was 1986 and the NY Giants were going to the Super Bowl. Everyone on the Trading Floors was amped up. The NY Giants were finally going to the Super Bowl it seemed so surreal since I had just met Coach Parcells and some of the players at camp the previous year. One of the owner's sons traded in the Pit where I was working. I had a connection to this game. NYC was crazier than ever over this game. Everyone in NY wanted to go. Tickets were a premium. I wanted to go but our bosses were all going we had to hold down the fort. I was finally starting to make real money. Instead of $180 a week I was now on salary and bonus. I guess I could afford to go but once again, I was a die hard JET Fan. Plus, this was a chance to prove I could pick up the slack and help run the business for the three days they were all away.

Being a native New Yorker, I was happy the Giants won. They had a ticker tape Parade on Broadway a block away from where I worked on Trinity Place in Lower Manhattan. I attended the parade on Broadway, which was awesome. The canyon of heroes! I attended at least 6 of the ticker tape parades while working in lower Manhattan. These Included the NY Rangers, NY Mets , NY Yankees, USA Olympians as well as the Armed Serviceman after the Gulf War. If you ever get the chance to attend one I would urge you to do so as they are truly epic.

Once the season is over most people forget about Football until the next August. Later in the year, I had received a promotion. I was made a member of the exchange and given a seat. It had been two and a half years since I started down there and finally all the hard work paid off. I was well on my way to becoming a partner in the firm. Everything was hitting on all cylinders until the October 19, 1987. The Stock Market crashed selling off 19% in one day.

After the Stock Market crashed sports and Super Bowls took a back seat to economic turmoil and job security. Money was tight, and it was about survival of the fittest. It wasn't until 1990 that things began to stabilize a bit.

Since 1969, I have been hearing about this game they call the Super Bowl. The older I became the closer I was getting to it. I went from hearing about Brooklyn Al bragging about being at every game to meeting actual players who participated in the game. Despite the economic chaos I had endured. I still pondered in the back of my mind about the big game. I started to wonder how would I ever "GET TO THE SHOW"?

Chapter 3 Juggling The Logistics

In 1990, we were in the middle of a recession. Basically, that's when the Economy Sucks. What do people turn to? They utilize Sports or any other form of entertainment that would distract you from the everyday pressures of living life. They need to escape reality for a couple of hours. In 1990, Over 80 Million people watched the Super Bowl in the USA. Internationally it was viewed in over 35 Countries. While only 80,000 fans get to attend. This pales in Comparison to the World Cup of Soccer which draws over 200 million viewers. It's a difficult ticket to get. How in the world would you even go about getting a ticket much less working out the logistics of getting to the game and securing hotel and dinner reservations? There was no Internet. Only a few people had cell phones which were big and bulky. Those who owned one were charged by the minute. There had to be a way a means of securing a ticket and finally getting to the Super Bowl. I just had to find it.

A lucky break happened later that year it was after Thanksgiving. One of my brother's former coach got a job as a coach for the Buffalo Bills. Luckily, he had kept in touch with this coach. We come to find out that tickets are distributed to NFL players and coaches. If you team is playing in the game, you receive more tickets than the other teams in the league. Eureka, we struck the Mother Lode!

We inquired if there was any way possible to buy two tickets at face value as the NFL allows. We would be forever grateful. This was the defining moment I've been waiting 21 years to see this game to be a part of history. I was finally getting closer. He said he really didn't want to jinx the team. Once they secured their spot in the Final Game he would let us know. During the season, the hot hand belonged to Jim Kelly the Buffalo Bills Quarterback. He and his teammates dominated, winning 90% of the team's games. They had a menacing defense led by Defensive End Bruce Smith the NFL Sack leader. All roads lead through Buffalo with its frigid temperatures in December and its Lake Effect snow. Earlier in the Season we had seen them crush my NY Jets in Giants Stadium at the Meadowlands. That's right Giant Stadium. The Jets are the only NFL Franchise that share a Home Stadium. No Wonder they can't get back to the SHOW they are the away team in their Home stadium!

In the NFC, the NY Giants were disposing of teams left and right. The road led through San

Francisco with their top ranked QB Joe Montana who dismantled the Miami Dolphins' team in Super Bowl XIX. I discussed the now famous 8-6 game earlier. In 1986, I couldn't attend the Super Bowl in Pasadena. Now I was getting closer to attending a Super Bowl. The game was scheduled to be in Tampa, Florida. There was a slight issue. The Gulf War had just started, and everyone was glued to their screens watching the War live on CNN. Would they cancel the game since we were at War?

Every week both the Giants and the Bills drew closer to a meeting with destiny in Tampa. We wouldn't know until the Bills won the AFC Championship whether we could get our hands on a pair of tickets. It was a waiting game. Time always goes so slow when you're at work or your anticipating something to occur, yet it seems to go so fast when you're on vacation.

We couldn't plan any other logistics until we secured the tickets. Without the ticket it was back to the Monticello Room to watch the game on TV like 80 million other viewers. It sounded regal the "Monticello Room". Surely Thomas Jefferson would be proud! It would be Standing Room only. If you got up to use the facilities, you were screwed till the next commercial break. As great as the memories of watching Super Bowls in that room, this was our big chance to Get to the Show!

Finally, Championship Sunday arrived the Bills had to beat the LA Raiders to advance. The previous year the Bills lost to the Cleveland Browns. By the final whistle the Bills beat the Raiders 51-3. The Bills were heavily favored to win the Super Bowl.

Over in the NFC the NY Giants had to defeat the San Francisco 49ers. They won a hard-fought Defensive battle 15-13. How in the world would they be able to match up against the explosive Bills Offensive machine? The Card was set for Super Bowl XXV January 27th in Tampa Florida.

We waited until Monday to call to congratulate the coach and his team on their blowout. Low and behold we secured two tickets. Ironically, it was an all-New York Super Bowl which left out my beloved NY Jets. The Curse was alive and well. The fact that my 21-year-old fascination with the Super Bowl was taking me to the next level of attending the Game allayed my annual disappointment in my beloved team. It had been over 20 years since I heard about Brooklyn Al and his wisecracking about going to the Game. Now I was finally getting to experience it in person. We had 5 days to figure out the logistics. We had to secure flights as close to Tampa as possible and hotel rooms. Remember this is pre-internet. There is no Kayak, Expedia, Priceline or Hotels.com. We put our two College educated heads together and began to see if we had any friends living in Florida. It turns out that my brother's teammate a running back worked at Disney, so we worked the phones to get airfare to Orlando and secure a room there.

Super Bowl host cities such as Miami or Tampa offer many more options then say a destination venue such as Minnesota last year. So, we knew we wouldn't have such a difficult time. The issue would be getting a hotel closer to Tampa the day of the game. You see the NFL and the Networks such as FOX, book out blocks of rooms or even the entire hotel for this event years in advance. So, the selection or choices you must consider become fewer. That's not even taking into consideration the huge increase in price or 3-day minimum stay the hotel owners price gouge you with.

We arrived in Orlando Friday evening and check into our Hotel just outside Disney. My brother calls Bill and he informs us to meet him at Pleasure Island the new Adult section of Disney. He is the manager of a Brand-New NYC style club there. We enter the elevator and are whisked up 5 flights. We get off on a cat walk which overlooks a rotating round dance floor. We scurry over the narrow catwalk like a pack of rats and descend the stairs. After ordering a drink, my brother asks for Bill and they promptly call him on the walkie talkie. He shows up comps our drinks and my brother and him catch up on old times.

At this point I mingle with the crowd and run into several NFL Players. Steve "Mongo" McMichael from the Chicago Bears Championship team. I go about 240 6'1 but I dwarfed in comparison. Then I ran in to Preston Pierson from the Dallas Cowboys a Hall of Famer. Who was famous for "The Hail Mary Catch" in a win over the Vikings in 1975. There were several other payers there. There was some linebacker from the Vikings, Joey badass or something. He was a bit obnoxious while the other players were cool about partying with the common folk.

At 12:30 Bill finally came back. I admitted to having some difficulty exiting the fast-moving dance floor after consuming a couple of cocktails. He reached into his pocket and pulled out a couple of pairs of cheap sunglasses. He instructed us to put them on. He said this was his favorite part of the job and walked over to a giant switch. It was a big U - shaped switch something you would see in a Frankenstein Movie as the monster was raised up and get hit with lightning.

The DJ announced last call and the dance floor grinded to a halt. That was his que. Bill sauntered over to the switch and lifted it up. With that came a collective groan from the inebriated patrons. Stadium lights illuminated the entire club. Until now we hadn't even noticed them against the blackened interior. He instructed the bouncer & bartender that we were his guests. Then they proceeded to herd out the stunned and temporarily blinded patrons. After a night cap in the empty club it was time to head back to the hotel.

I finally lay my head down, after laughing about recapping the night. I could only imagine what was in store for us the next two days.

We rented a midsize car and began our 85-mile trek to Tampa. We used the Map Avis gave us and drew co-encentric circles around Tampa 15 miles, 25 miles, & 50 miles. (Millennials a map is made of Paper there was no GPS or Google maps) Our plan was to locate two hotel chains that we spotted along the way. We would first stop at hotels 60 miles out and book a room. As we got 40 miles out we would book that room if available then cancel the previous one we had booked. We basically leap frogged until we got to Tampa. Each circle radius was smaller than the last. We had secured our last hotel about 30 miles out and decided to drive into Tampa to ascertain the whereabouts of the stadium in relationship of the city and neighboring towns. In certain cities, the NFL stadiums are right smack in the middle of the downtown metro area. In NY, both teams play 15 miles outside city limits, in the Meadowlands, or the former swamps of New Jersey. In Boston, the stadium is 40 minutes south in Foxboro, Massachusetts. Ironically, it's closer to Rhode Island.

We pulled up to this hotel and it had a HUGE Banner that read Buffalo Bills Headquarters. Outside in the parking lot they had the biggest tent I had ever seen. Bigger than a Ringling Brother's Circus Tent. I walked to front desk I asked what was the tent for? She said it was for the Victory party. I figured I'd toss her a softball question first. Then I had the balls to ask her if she had a room available tonight. She laughed said this was booked by the owner Buffalo Bills Ralph Wilson a year ago. It was an average hotel, but the place was bustling with activity. Just then another young lady came from behind the office door at the desk. She overheard our conversation and stated they had one cancellation. Are you kidding me? So excited I Fumbled to get my wallet open and retrieve my credit card, I yelled I'll take it. Never in a million years did I expect to get a room in Tampa no less at Buffalo Bills Headquarters. We had the room behind the front desk they were using its to store glassware for the Victory Celebration. All night long we heard carts going by stocking the tent with everything you needed for a Victory Celebration! Our Mission was complete we arrived safely, secured lodging in the hosting city 10 miles from the Tampa Stadium and we had two tickets, we were finally "GETTING TO THE SHOW".

Chapter 4 CALM Before The STORM

We woke up and it wasn't a dream. I drew back the curtains and low and behold our room on the first floor had the most incredible view. Rubbing the sandman out of my eyes, I saw this glorious parking lot filled with cars from NY all with Buffalo Bills red blue and white banners and flags. It wasn't a dream we were in Buffalo Bills Headquarters. We showered and headed out to grab some food. It was too late for Breakfast, so we found a local Fish restaurant and ate lunch. Next it was on to see Tampa Stadium. It was a sunny day about 75 degrees. As we exited the highway, we could see this gigantic saddle shaped stadium towering into the blue sky. We circled the parking lots which were heavily secured and scanned to see what gate we would enter. The anticipation was building.

My brother had called his former coach who had asked us to meet him outside Tampa at one of his favorite BBQ joints. He frequented this smoked pork & beef mecca while on his college recruiting trips. It was basically a log cabin type shack where the meats were smoked in pits out back. The pungent hickory smoke wafted through the back of restaurant. It was family style and we sat at picnic tables. We ordered whatever the coach suggested and began to feast on Carolina style pulled pork & Texas Style Brisket. Baked beans and coleslaw garnished our plates. Washing it all down with Sweet Tea. Anything more than two glasses you could go into diabetic shock. I swear it had twice as much sugar in there then a can of soda.

The Coach was a former player himself. Like the rest of us he gained a few pounds after his playing days. But you could still see there was power in his frame and arms if he ever summoned it. He was an affable stout man with a good personality. My brother would tell me stories how he strolls the sidelines and sing this song just prior to going full speed in certain drills or practice.

He was the Defensive Line Coach. His toughest, biggest, Defensive line man would go one on one against my brother's Offensive lineman. At first, he couldn't understand him with his drawl and a chew of tobacco. But later he would laugh when he heard him start to sing and come to expect it. By the time he was a Junior they dominated and handily dispensed his Defensive squad.

After about two hours we picked up the check and paid him face value for our tickets. We thanked and wished him the best on Sunday. We hopped in our car and headed back to the hotel. Back at the lobby it was bustling. Boosters, Fans and Family members flooded the in-house bar and restaurant. They were so happy, it was as if they had already won. They weren't arrogant or cocky they were good hearted people from upstate New York. Some of the nicest people you would ever want to meet. My three brothers and I all attended college upstate New York. We had great experiences with the local people. They were predominantly hardworking, honest, family-oriented folk that would give you the shirt off your back if you needed it. They were the opposite of the jaded type you came across while working in New York City. I'm not sure if it's the clean country air & water, the Rural vibe or the wide-open country that produces such attitudes. But the comparison between upstate and downstate people in New York is noticeably different.

We were sitting in the Catbird Seat. We couldn't lose. We were attending our first Super Bowl. Either way it was a win -win situation for us. A New York team would be crowned Champs. True, If the Giants won we would be happier. But if the Bills won we would be ground zero for one of the best celebrations ever! We went back to the room to shower up and get ready to walk across the street to the infamous Yucatan Liquor Stand.

My brother showered as I watched the news. It was a bit of a reality check. The USA was still at war with Iran. We were in the middle of Operation Desert Storm. The previous August, Saddam Hussein and his National Guard had invaded the small Oil rich Country of Kuwait. Citizens of Kuwait had the highest per capita wealth of anyone in the World.

The rebels set oil fields on fire. Although the US retaliation was surely to end this war relatively quickly, it was the beginning of a new age of Terrorism.

When the news switched to sports it reported about the Super Bowl being a possible target. Fans would not be allowed to bring in bags or cameras. There would be several security checkpoints and to allow yourself three hours prior to the game to get into the stadium. Suddenly, the outside World gave us a dose of reality. I remembered the 1977 movie Black Sunday where terrorists flew a blimp into the Stadium. Good old liberal Hollywood giving our enemies ideas again. I worried for a bit then realized the security would be tight and the probability of something happening would be minimal. You see I always was in the camp that terrorism usually need an element of surprise to be successful. They also go after unarmed citizens instead of confronting the heavily armed military. Tampa Stadium was in full lock down.

After the commercials they cut live to a local Italian Restaurant I believe to be owned by Vinny Testaverde. He was the great University of Miami and NFL Quarterback who played for an amazing 21 seasons. He came up one game short in leading my NY Jets to the Super Bowl in 1991. They interviewed Steve De Berg the present-day Quarterback for the Hometown Tampa Bay Buccaneers. He gave a lively interview and they cut to a commercial.

It was time to go across the street and celebrate our accomplishments. We were now 20 hours away from attending our first Super Bowl. The Yucatan Liquor Stand was enormous. It was a combination of outside patios and an inside dining area. It probably held about 1000 people or more. It was a 15-minute wait just to get in. We walked around the place there was a band inside and another outside. We settled smack in the middle on an outside deck. It was a crossroad of the entire place everyone had to go through the middle to visit the inside or get to the bathrooms. After about 10 minutes I recognize an old friend Bobby Leavy who I played ball with in HS. I had heard he had retired from the NY Fire Department and moved to Florida. He said the Donatello brothers were also down for the game. I had played with the second oldest and my younger brothers played with theirs. We exchanged salutations and the drinking picked up its pace. These guys were all big dudes and there we all stood right there in the middle with everyone just going around us to get inside.

Ironically, Steve DeBerg shows up with his father in law in tow. I never would have recognized him if I just hadn't seen him on the local news. We say hello introduce everyone and he has a couple of beers with us. I tell him I saw him on the news. I said you must have had a couple at the restaurant. He laughed then caught himself and inquired if he sounded inebriated. I dispelled his fears saying I was just busting his chops. You did great and assured him that he could have a future in broadcasting once he retired. Just then, some weasel comes up and asks him about a game five years ago and why didn't they run out the clock instead of throwing a late pic six. He gives the weasel a blank stare. Turning to us he says his goodbyes before disappearing sea of people.

We continue to drink tell old stories about growing up on the "ROCK" (Staten Island. It's about 11:30 now and the place is getting extremely crowded. Some idiot forces his way between our group. One of the Donatello brother shoots him a look. The *wannnabee* tough guy was tall with some tattoos and a goatee. When gets about 20 feet away he turns and curses us out. It always amazes me how brave people become the further away they get! We were there to have fun and talk about Football. We couldn't be bothered by some drunk fool.

The lines were 5-deep at the Porta Johns, I took care of business when I heard some sirens. I stepped outside only to learn that the Fire Marshall was shutting the place down of overcapacity code violations. It was a massive sea of people. I searched in vain for my brother to no avail. I started to head back to the Hotel when I ran into my crew from the Rock. They invite me to go with them into Mons Venus the infamous strip club. I entered the Mammary Mecca with its strobe lights and blaring music. The place was packed with scantily clothed large breasted woman gyrating on poles and dancing on tables. I was on a budget and didn't exactly have a lot of expendable cash to throw away on girls that I didn't see anything remotely positive in the future with. Besides at this point I had consumed enough alcohol to make a citizen's arrest on myself as "Otis the Drunk". Time to exit stage left.

I decided to call it a night and bid farewell to my crew. I stumbled a couple of blocks back to the hotel. I made it back to the room and struggled to get the key to work. My brother was lying the bed and inquired what happened. After catching up trading stories we both realized we were starving we attempted to get some chow at the bar in the hotel. While walking across the lobby we noticed a commotion. There was a large stretch Lincoln limousine with a couple of drunks being kicked out of it. Two of the people remaining in the Limo bared a striking resemblance to Football Players. WTF? It's the night before their biggest game could they have broken curfew? Maybe I was seeing things. We stood there in disbelief for what seemed like an hour. We looked at each other and at that very moment we both said the same thing we must bet the GIANTS! There was no way Parcells would let any of his players out the night before the biggest game of the year or their careers. He was a tough disciplinarian as my brother had found out first hand as a ball boy for the Giants. The Buffalo Players were as sure as the fans that they would win. They beat their last opponent 51-3. Surely, they would lay an old-fashioned ass whooping on the Giants. But they always have to play the game.

By the time we walked into the restaurant, the kitchen was closed. I paid the price as I woke up with severe hangover the next morning. We had to get up hydrate and plan the final stage of our journey. It's now 8 hours till kickoff.

Chapter 5 Game Day

Battling a hangover, I attempted to hydrate, stay out of the Sun and get some solid food in me. I would probably be one of the few fans not sucking down stadium beer during the game. It was about 3 o'clock when we scammed a ride on the Buffalo Bills shuttle to the stadium. There were local Cops, State Police and National Guard. We got through Checkpoint Alpha unscathed. We disembarked the bus and began to walk around the stadium. There were huge tents set up for parties and the NFL Experience. Unfortunately, you needed to have separate tickets to get inside any of these venues. The sun was hot felt like 100 degrees and 90% humidity with no breeze. Perfect conditions to exacerbate ones Hangover. I just didn't have the patience to try and crash these parties. Besides, we had the only ticket that mattered. We were about to join 79,998 lucky fans to watch from inside this massive saddle shaped Tampa Bay Stadium.

It was about 3:30 when we decided to go through the final two checkpoints. We were scanned with wands and passed through metal detectors. There was one more line that wound around the stadium like a giant serpent and we were on the end of it. We baked in the Sun as we cursed the terrorists that caused all this added stress and disruption. They served Domino's Pizza on line if you wanted one for about 12 bucks. I sucked down water or Pepsi every chance I had.

Focus, hydrate and keep moving through the final checkpoint.

It was about 5:15 when we finally entered and found our seats on the second level with all the Buffalo Bills fans. I felt like was going to puke. What a rookie mistake! My first Super Bowl and I was hungover like a Bowery Bum. I decided to take a walk in the Stadium which was filling up slowly. In the Corner of the end zone the TV cameras were set up. I Believe it was the Monday Night Football Crew that were scheduled to Announce the game. On the Field I could see Frank Gifford, Dan Dierdorf and Al Michaels. Two out of three weren't bad.

The vibrant green turf was meticulously manicured. You could even smell the freshness of the last cut! The infield had about 100 white wooden chairs set up for an Orchestra. Whitney Houston was scheduled to sing the Star-Spangled Banner. It was becoming more real as the adrenaline began to flow. It was now an hour before the game players were starting to warm up. I worked my way back to my seat and hydrated some more. Like ants back to their anthill fans began to filter in more steadily and the empty seats were fewer to be seen.

Now things moved at a faster pace, the players went back into the locker room. There were several announcements. Instead of blimps or small planes trailing banners there were Apache attack Helicopters circling above. The fans began to cheer. We were the only two Giants fans in the whole Buffalo Bills section. We placed a $200 wager on the underdog NY Giants. Even though we were firmly entrenched behind enemy lines. We discussed how we can't root for the Giants and must cheer every time the Bills score. We couldn't let these passionate fans know that we were rooting against them. After all, without their coach we would be ticketless and back viewing the game in the Monticello Room!

Everything starts to a stream together as the starting players were announced after exiting the tunnel. The loud thundering rotors of the Apache Helicopters could be heard as they circled above. Then the announcement to stand for the National Anthem. There was a live Orchestra adorned in Tuxedos on the field. They played a quick intro before Whitney Houston took the stage. She began softly like an angel only to Finish like Athena the "Greek God of War" in what has been described to this day as the best rendition of our National Anthem ever!!! The Hair was standing up om the back of my neck. I Had tears in my eyes. The Navy Fighter Jets buzzed the stadium, the crowd began to chant USA...USA...USA to a fever pitch. This was Superbowl XXV the cost of a ticket was $200, Plane Tickets & Lodging $1400, the cost of a 30 second TV Spot was $800,000. Sharing the Super Bowl experience with my Youngest Brother was Priceless!

10-9-8-7.... The Coin Toss then two NY Teams with identical 13-3 regular season records were about to do epic battle. By halftime the offensive powerhouse Bills were held to a lackluster 12 points while the Giants trailed after scoring 10. Few people recall that the Defensive Coach for the Giants was the relatively unknown Bill Belichick. He had devised a tactical game of keep away. Run the Ball & Run the Clock. Keep the Bills Great Quarterback Jim Kelly and their no huddle offense on the Sideline while they ate up the clock. This ingenious plan would present the Giants the best opportunity for victory. If the plan worked, they would upset one of the best offenses in NFL history. The first half was over. The Giants, led by back up QB Jeff Hostetler, controlled the ball almost 19 of the first 30 minutes of the game.

It was half time, contrary to the pundits our underdog Giants was still in this thing. I began to feel nauseous again. It wasn't from the hangover it was from the New Kids on the Block halftime show! We went into the tunnel to rustle up some food. My brother was sitting next to the coach's wife. When we got back his young son probably about 4, started to eat my brother's French fries. Crawling all over him like he was in the sandbox. He offered try to buy them some food and the kid chooses cotton-candy. By the end of the 3rd quarter. I look over and my brother shirt is covered in Pink Cotton Candy. Lol.

Finally, the second half begins, the Giants march down the field 75 yards. Eating up the clock as running back OJ Anderson scores a Touchdown. Two series later, defensive end Bruce Smith tackles the Giants running back Anderson on

4th down. Shortly after, the Bills running back Thurman Thomas scores a Touchdown on a 34yard scamper. Buffalo regains the lead 19-17. Back and Forth the game teetered. The Giants stuck to their game plan. On the Giants final possession, they kick a field goal and take the lead 20-19. We continue sit there in Bills Country and act like we don't care when the NY Giants score. Now it's the final opportunity for the Buffalo Bills. They get the ball on their own 10-Yard line. They need to gain about 65 yards to give their kicker a shot at a game winning Field Goal.

With 2:19 remaining in the game, the Bills offense takes the field and march to the Giants 29 Yard line. With time running out and 8 seconds left on the clock the Bills kicker comes out to kick the go-ahead game winning field goal. To figure out the length of a field goal you take the line of scrimmage and add 17 yards. This a combination of 10 yards in the end zone and the amount that the kicker is back from the line of scrimmage (7 Yards). It's a 47-Yard field goal to win the game. Now we are in Slow Motion. The snap is good the kick is up. Where we were sitting it was difficult to see if the kick was good or not. We had a bad angle. We could see that it was tailing off from our vantage point on the far side of the stadium. The Bills fans were jumping up and down as if it was good. We didn't care because the Giants covered the spread and we were about to go to an epic Victory Party!

Then we noticed Giant Players celebrating and we realized he had missed it by inches. Wide Right by less than a yard. Two teams 13-3 and it comes down to an epic chess match and an 8-second walk off field goal. Wide Right! My brother tried to explain to the coach's wife what just occurred, but the noise was deafening. I'm not sure she could comprehend that they had lost. Maybe she just didn't want to accept this heartbreaking loss. After spending 4 hours in enemy territory we both agreed it was time to exit stage left. By the closing Whistle, the NY Giants controlled the ball over 42 minutes. Neither team turned the football over. Outside the stadium it was pure bedlam a mixture of ebullient Giant fans and suicidal Bills fans. It took us about an hour to get back to the Hotel. In the cab on the way back my brother said he thought that was the best Super Bowl ever played. I said I'm not sure about that, but it was one of the best games I have ever seen in my lifetime.

Back at the Hotel it was eerily silent. The boisterous fans were nowhere to be found. Plenty of people were crying and hugging as they tried to console each other in this massive disappointment. How could their explosive Offense be stymied to only score 19 points? We entered the room turned on the 11 o'clock news . The lead off story was the "Best Super Bowl ever played!" All that preparation, all that food and booze that rattled by our room night and day. What would happen? I went back into the lobby again it felt like I was at a wake. The sadness was palatable. Then one by one players began to show up some on crutches others with ice packs. They all began to funnel down the hall to that huge tent that was set up for their Victory Party. In a testament to the human spirt and good sportsmanship they showed up at Buffalo Bills Headquarters Hotel. They were bruised & battle scared. It reminded me of an old movie where the Gladiators of Ancient Rome exit the Colosseum. Even though they were extremely disappointed and physically exhausted they all gathered together to regroup. They shared their pain of falling one game short. The emotional highs came crashing down with 8 seconds left. The finality of it all was gut wrenching.

Over the remainder of the decade, the Buffalo Bills continued to be successful under Head Coach Marv Levy. They would go on to play in 4 Super Bowls in total, over a short span of 7-years. Unfortunately, they never came out on the winning end in any of them. Regardless of their redundancy of losing their last game, several of their players walked into Canton Ohio on their first ballot. Bruce Smith, Jim Kelly, Thurman Thomas, James Lofton, Andre Reed and Head Coach Marv Levy. They were an incredibly exciting team to watch. They just came up a yard short.

Chapter 6 Back to The Grind

It's Monday morning, was it a dream or did we just witness the Best Super Bowl ever played? The Underdog NY Giants upset the Buffalo Bills by one point to win Super Bowl XXV. The Tampa newspaper had it splashed all over the front page and then some. We went into the lobby to get breakfast it was a ghost town. We were one of 3 tables eating the Buffalo Bills special two eggs easy over (kind of ironic), side of bacon, white toast and a bloody Mary with a chicken wing.

We were happy that we won our bet and the NY Giants won their 2nd Super Bowl in 5 years. If only it had been my beloved and much maligned NY Jets. Someday I dreamed. In either case my 20-year quest to "Get to the Show" had all but ended. Was this my 15 minutes of fame that Andy Warhol had written about? The experience was truly amazing! The things I enjoyed the most besides the game, were the sense of adventure and the spontaneity of it all. Meeting old friends as well as the athletes was a surprise we never planned on. The fact that we accomplished all the logistics within 5 days is a testament to old fashion ingenuity. After all, the NFL and the Networks plan these games 2-years in advance. The amount of tourism dollars to the area surrounding the stadium has to be in the 100's of millions.

There was a lot to digest and process. So much had transpired in such short time span. We had time to get back to Orlando as we had booked a night flight. We decided to take one more look at that beautiful saddle shaped arena were the gladiators did battle just 12 hours earlier. Workers were busy dismantling the tents and other temporary structures. It really is an amazing fete to organize and put on such a quality experience for all the football fans.

We noticed an army of rental trucks scurrying around the stadium. We saw one being loaded up with souvenirs. We decided to follow the full truck to see where the central collection area was. Being native New Yorkers, we knew the souvenirs were going to be discounted and some could even "Fall off the Truck". That's an old Brooklyn term where things go missing in the rail or shipyards. It later morphed into hijacking the entire truck. Most of the time the drivers were in on it. In the 1970's gangs would hijack trucks of cigarettes and put them in the vending machines in local bars and bowling alleys. Occasionally, they would get raided as the pack of cigarettes didn't have any tax stamps. In 1975, cigarettes cost 75 cents a pack compared to present day price of $15 dollars a pack in NYC. Even back then the government added a 10% tax on them.

We followed the truck to a storage unit where everything was being dumped off. We exit the car and approached the crew. I blurted out this was their lucky day and proceeded to sift through the shirts, jerseys and discounted souvenirs. What a score we loaded up two bags and handed over $100 bucks. There was an Ice bucket made from a real NFL commemorative helmet. We tried to get it for $50 bucks it was originally $300. They wouldn't part with it. So off we went on our 85-mile ride back to Orlando.

The trip back was anticlimactic and boring. We came, we saw, we conquered. Now it was back to reality. Back to waking up at 5:30 and taking the BUS to NYC to work 10 hours then return home. We had incredible memories that most people would only dream of. On the plane ride home, I pondered Would I ever "Get back to the Show?"

Upon reflection, I'd say it pays to stay in touch with old friends, teachers and coaches. You never know when your paths may cross again. We pulled off an incredible trip to the Super Bowl that would have cost over $5000 dollars. We couldn't afford to book this trip through a travel agent. By thinking outside the box with a positive attitude it all came together.

My one regret is that we didn't have any pictures. Cameras weren't allowed inside the stadium as they posed a security threat. Cell phones with cameras hadn't been invented yet.

Chapter 7 One If By Land, Two If By Sea

The next few years I was transitioning from a Floor Trader/Specialist to an "upstairs" Trader/ Analyst. We were in the middle of a Recession, I was out of work for 10 months. I was in survival mode. Instead of becoming a millionaire by the time I was 30 I was struggling. I divested assets. I gave a condo and a Summer house back to the banks. There was no Obama bailout back then. I had to reinvent myself if I was going to make a viable career on Wall St.

Over the years, traders always asked my opinion on what direction individual equities or the Market itself was headed. I had become an excellent Technical Analyst that interpreted charts better than most. I devised systems that would monitor and scan stocks for any sign of reversals whether up or down. I threw myself into my work. Spending 10 hours a day or more looking for the slightest edge. I started my own company TRENDWATCH and was a frequent guest on Television. I guest appeared on the financial segments on CNBC, FNN and Bloomberg for seven years. Phoenix rose from the ashes! I had a new career on Wall Street!

It was the second time I had to take a step backwards to eventually move forwards and up the corporate ladder. This time it was extremely painful as I had lost all the equity in both homes and basically everything that I had toiled so hard for.

It was now 1996, six years since Super Bowl 25. I was 34 years old I was making $250,000 a year. I had moved to a small town in a condo right on the Navesink River in NJ. My friend Mike was a Lobsterman who had moved there a year earlier. He informed me there was a high-speed ferry to Wall St NYC. I went up to investigate and moved in. Every morning I rose at 5:15. Showered dressed and walked approximately 150 feet from my front door to get on the Sea Streak Ferry a massive Steel Catamaran hulled vessel that held about 220 people. It had two levels with bathrooms, theater style seating and low and behold a horseshoe shaped bar. It roared through the water at speeds up to 28 Knots. It was about 28 nautical miles by sea to NYC compared to 42 miles by land. Best of all there was no crammed bus, no traffic waiting to go through tunnels or over bridges. It was 3 times as expensive. It was $420 a month but it was well worth it.

I knew no one on the ferry. Zero Zippo not a soul. I rode the 6:15 AM ferry. It was nicknamed the "Over Achiever Boat." There was also a 7:20 then an 8:15. Three boats you missed one then you waited an hour. Little by little I'd get the hang of the routine and I'd make an acquaintance or two here or there. This was a boat full of "Type A" personalities and large egos. Most were extremely wealthy Wall Streeters, Lawyers or CEO's. They would walk by you as if you didn't exist. If you talked to them they would ignore you. It would be a tough crowd to ever break into. Why would you even want to?

I had been riding for about two months. It was a Monday I was tired from the weekend. I decided I needed to sit down. Most of the seats were full so I opened the hatch door walked outside and climbed up the stairwell to the second level. We were about to get under way. I spied a seat at a table that sat 4 passengers. I took a seat across from a lady in her mid- thirties. I wasn't sure if was an eye roll or side eye. But she surely made me uncomfortable. Shortly after that two well-dressed gentlemen approached and asked if they could squeeze in. I had never seen them before, but she knew both and greeted them by name. They were real smug looking the one who sat next to me looked like a young Clark Gable with phoniest laugh I had ever heard. The other gentleman Harry thanked Tiff for getting up. They all had nicknames. They weren't the normal Blue-Collar ones I was accustomed to such as Mikee, Sallyboy or Tommy. It was Tiff and Harold and Blaire. It was a table for 4 people but to them there was only 3 sitting there. I'm hard to miss at 240 and 6'1 but they managed to ignore me. It was if the seat was vacant. Tiff opened a white waxed paper bag the kind they give you at a French bakery. She puts a muffin on a plate and cuts into three pieces. She puts out her index finger circles the muffin and looks me straight in the eye and says this is for "OUR LITTLE GROUP". I looked at her and had all to do to keep my tongue in my mouth. Instead I starred right through her. Should I be happy that she finally acknowledged my existence? Should I be disappointed that I had moved into a new neighborhood full of a "bunch of tools?" The Brooklyn in me wanted to rip them all to shreds with their designer attire and smugness. I refrained. I sat there failing to acknowledge her spoiled child like demeanor. I wouldn't give her the satisfaction of getting a rise out of me. I read the newspaper cover to cover. I was slow to get up when we approached the Wall Street dock. I could feel their frustration as I took my time getting up. After all I was the new kid on the block this was their territory, and this is how they played their clique games. It was pathetic. It was that very moment that I realize they attempted to show their superiority to me. I was better than the lot of them and I'd go on to prove it. After that experience, it was months before I ever sat down again,

One weekend I went to Princeton for a charity benefit with my roommate and his brother, I was introduced to a fellow by the name of Mike Tucker Aka TUCK from here on out. He grew up in my new neighborhood and pretty much new everyone. He was an upstairs market maker for Cantor Fitzgerald. He was about 6t'2 200 pounds he had played Hockey at Christian Brothers Academy CBA and attended school upstate at Syracuse. He was recently married and had just welcomed his first child. We discovered the similar education backgrounds and both our penchant for busting people's balls. He was one of the funniest guys I had ever met. I was fortunate that he took a liking to me and he introduced me to everyone. He became one of my best friends. I believe that without him I never would have been as successful as quickly I as I had. He would take me out to client dinners, in exchange I'd send him charts and monitor his pad of stocks that he made markets in. Soon customers that he had introduced me to were paying me monthly. He invited me to play golf at his club, to his beach club and to his daughters 2nd Birthday. He became one of my best friends. However, if you ever slipped up or gave him an opening. He would bust your balls like no other.

I remember going to his house in Rumson, NJ. I was driving an old Buick Riviera. I purposely parked a block away, so I wouldn't give him the opportunity to make fun of my car. Caddy's and this type of Buick were usually driven by Guido's (a slang for Italians from Staten Island or Brooklyn. Now to be clear, it wasn't that I was ashamed of where I grew up as I always have been "comfortable in my own skin". I never particularly cared what anyone ever thought of me. I just knew that you had to be careful to give him any ammo. He could be brutal. He was the master of cutting some down and busting their balls. He would hold court at the Ferry bar. He could be a Pitbull. If you took the ribbing to personally, he would realize it and put his arm around you and say "take it easy Janney Sensitive" I'm only kidding. He was extremely generous, always buying drinks for the crew.

The next year I bought a Lincoln Continental. The ad in the paper read: 1990 Champagne Lincoln Continental 4 door sun roof leather interior new tires 56,000 miles. I bought the car for $5500. At least this was a bit more of a respectable car. It was a classier version of the town cars we took home from the city after a night of drinking. The parking lot at the ferry was full of Mercedes, Range Rovers and Beemer's. At least this car was in better shape than the banged-up Buick.

It was a Wednesday or Thursday and Tuck called me at work. The call started as usual, Jackass what's up? What's new haven't heard from you this week. I made the mistake of telling him I bought a new car well not new but newer used car. He said congrats what you get? I said a Lincoln Continental. Now traders talk fast especially when they have very few moments to talk during the business day. One missed call or trade could cost you thousands in seconds. So, it's usually rapid fire, short sound bites then click back to business. The next rapid-fire words out of his mouth were: what color? Without thinking I spit out the answer CHAMPAGNE. There was a pause. Right then and there I knew I was dead! I had given him a whole truck of AMMO. It was that split second where the brain answers and before you can shut your trap the words spill out. He said Champagne WTF? I could hear him laughing. He invited me to meet him after work at Johnny's Fish Grill across from the Trade Center. We were going to the Aircraft Carrier Intrepid as Cantor Fitzgerald had rented it out for a party.

I knew I was dead. He must have called 20 guys bust Langan's balls about the Champagne Lincoln. What was I thinking. Who the hell puts Champagne in an ad as a color. I was dead. If the under/ over was 100 on how many times someone would bust my balls. You got paid if you took the over. This went on for years.

I was now officially part of his crew. We never sat on the ferry we always stood up by the bar. We basically stood for 45 minutes since we sat at desks all day for 9 hours. It was the reverse of the guys who worked on the floor they were members or clerks they stood up for 9 hours. Ironically, they had seats on the exchange, but it was just a term or slang for their membership. Everyone stood 90% of the day.

On the boat there were several cliques. Across the bar were the "shemps" slang for the 5th Stogia that no one cared for. The infamous slapstick comedy troupe, "The Three Stooges" were comprised of Mo, Larry and Curly. Occasionally Joe would sit in. If they were desperate they gave

"Shemp" the nod. It was basically the second-string stooges. Think of this analogy, it's kind of the Washington Generals to the World-Famous Harlem Globetrotters.

So finally, I met some good guys who I had some things in common with. In the morning I'd see them we'd discuss the previous day's trading, sports or local events that were going on. When the boat docked we all disembarked first as we were stood right by the door. Next in line were a group of about 25 older businessman 40-60-year-old seasoned vets. We were just an obstacle for them to get off the boat. Once off the boat, I walked with this crew up Wall St. Some peeled off at the New York Stock Exchange NYSE while others forged on. At Broadway under the shadow of the Trinity Church I headed underground to take the subway uptown. While Tuck and his posse headed west to the World Trade Center.

I took the Subway up to 57st got off and walked back down to 51st and 3rd where my office was. This added another $4 dollars to my trip and added at least 35 minutes of my morning commute between added walking and the Subway ride. This quickly got old. After about two months, I began to realize that the older crew behind us exhibited more wisdom than previously thought. Once they disembarked downtown, they walked to Water St and climbed into waiting cabs. Instead of riding the ferry to midtown, they disembarked. It was a well-oiled machine almost like a military operation. Three or Four to a cab and they sped up the FDR Drive to go to midtown. The cab would beat the ferry uptown where it was harder to hail a cab. Then it would drop off everybody at or close to their office. This was ingenious. I could pay a dollar more than the Subway and be in my office 25 minute earlier as the cabs were always going against the traffic flow in the morning. Finally, a clique I wanted to be accepted into.

My Apartment in Highlands, New Jersey was riverfront. The Navesink River was 60 feet from my door. The Ferry dock was 50 yards or so from my front door. One minute before they took off they would blow the horn. I could still jog down stairs and across the blacktop pick up a newspaper from Charlie and still make the boat with time to spare. Talk about convenience! The other commuters had to drive from the surrounding towns and park in this oversized lot owned by this turn of the century old Connor's Hotel. In the morning, I'd watch the commuters file into the ferry, first a trickle then a crowd. I noticed that the first one on around 5:50 was an older balding man built like a linebacker. He would sit in the first booth and watch everyone the Ferry. He was the Type A of Type A's. The King of the Over achiever Boat. This guy had to get up at 4:45 shower drive from west Rumson and still be on the boat before anyone. Sometimes he would even beat crew members. My pattern recognition skills were working on other things besides stocks.

The next morning, I inquired about him with Tucks crew. They were dismissive and didn't have anything good to say. After about another week of walking up Wall St and going into the hot subway to get uptown and walking again to my office I had all but had it. On the way home, that night I began to wonder why my new crew didn't have a good opinion of the newly crowned Type A leader. I think they weren't happy about him and his legion crowding around the bar as we drew closer to the Wall St. dock. Then I realized two things. First, not one of Tuck's crew traveled uptown. Secondly, why was I listening to people's opinion of another person? I had always lived my life not to listen to drama or BS but to formulate my own opinion about every individual I meet.

I formulated a plan. It was a steamy day in August, most people try to get in last minute vacations before Summer slips away. I knew what I wanted to say, and the timing was right.
I walked over to his table, the conversation abruptly ended. You could hear a pin drop. I felt 4 pairs of eyes glaring at me. Would this be a repeat of Tiff and the Muffin gang?

I leaned over and put out my hand to introduce myself. I said: Mr. Cunningham, my name is Stephen Langan I work at 51st and 3rd. I see that you meticulously organize all the rides uptown on bar napkins early each morning. If there's ever an empty seat or you need a rider to fill up a cab I'd greatly appreciate it if you would include me. There was silence. He got up from the booth as were coming around Governors Island. The he finally spoke. He said today you ride with me "Big Guy" and slapped me on the back. He said my name is Bill, but my friends call me Coach. I was in shock! I was expecting a no, or I'll keep you in mind. But a yes and to ride with the man who devised this genius plan. I just hit the jackpot. I was in my office at 6:55 that day.

Everyday I'd stand at the bar. When coach got up I made sure he had a clear path to the door. I'd ask who am I riding with? He would yell out today you're with Billy and John. Three of us in a Cab $4 bucks each and off we went. Coach turned out to be one of the best guys I met on that boat that I rode for 14 years. He was a Bond trader who did a lot of business in Asia. He would spend about a month overseas each year. Over time I came to find out that he played Football down in Asbury Park NJ then became a Referee for High School & College. People still called him Coach instead of Ref. One Thursday I'm in the cab with him and he starts talking about the Football Season and how he wouldn't be around on Fridays. That was the day I realized not only was he still reffing, but he was a Referee in the NFL. He would explain he was part of a crew and never knew what city or what game they had until Friday morning. I believe the NFL used this cloak of secrecy to prevent any shenanigans with gamblers trying to have access to the refs. Not only was Coach one of the 7 refs on the field he was the Field Judge positioned right behind the Linebackers. Plain and simple During the week he played “Uptown Ferry Rider Soduko” organizing rides on Sunday he was a badass in the defensive backfield.

It was December 1996, midweek I was riding in a cab uptown with Coach and John. I asked Coach if he ever reffed a Super Bowl. He said not yet but he hoped this was his year. I had told him I was at the Super Bowl XXV Giants vs Buffalo Game. The he said he had been to so many games but was really anticipating to finally ref the biggest game of his life. He was also trying to “GET TO THE SHOW” but in different capacity. Over the years he forged many friendships with other refs and owners of teams. I then asked him if he gets tickets to the SHOW. He said: yes, all players, coaches & refs get access to tickets and he gets two. I replied: well if you ever get them and don’t want to us them I’d love to go again. I offered to buy them face value as the rules allow. He said: if I don’t get the Superbowl this year I’ll get you two. I couldn’t thank him enough and told him I’d still be rooting for him to get to Ref the Big Game.

I didn’t want to tell anyone or get my hope up. It was January, NFL Championship Sunday was this week. I wouldn’t see coach until the following Tuesday. The Super Bowl was being played in

Superdome on Jan 26, 1997. I had more time to plan since the Championship games were on January 12, 1997. There was a two-week layoff between games. But hey, it wasn't my first Rodeo. I watched both games. Green Bay with Brett Favre at the helm, beat the Carolina Panthers 30-13. The New England Patriots now being Coached by two-time Super Bowl winner with the NY Giants Bill Parcells. They beat the Jacksonville Jaguars 20-6. The Final Game of the season was an excellent match-up between the New England Patriots and the Green Bay Packers who hadn't won a Super Bowl since Lombardi died. Ironically, the Super Bowl trophy is named after him and this was the Packers chance to bring it back home. This would be one heck of a game.

Tuesday, I get in the cab with coach and he hands me an envelope. I peak inside and see two Super Bowl Tickets. I was speechless for a second it was bitter sweet. After all, the Coach deserved to finally Ref the big game, but it wasn't in the cards this year. His let down opened the door for my opportunity for a repeat visit to the SHOW. It speaks volumes about his character that he held true to his word. He instructed me to write a check for the exact face value amount. I regained my composure and thanked him profusely.

If I had listened to my crew I never would have met Coach. I'd still be walking and taking the crowded Subway. I never would have had the opportunity to partake in all those cab ride conversations, which led up to me attending my second Super Bowl. The lesson I had learned long ago held fast. You be the one to judge a person's character. Don't listen to other's opinions! You are intelligent enough to formulate your own opinions and draw your own conclusions.

Chapter 8 Down On The Bayou

I have tickets in hand. The most important piece of the puzzle. Now I had a new tool the fledgling internet. Dial up service sounds u never heard before "*cruuuuzzzz Zing xlll oooo ngggg ooohhh crshhh znnnggg*" you are connected AOL. Dial up Internet was a step up from the phone book and cell phones were becoming more prominent. The Motorola Flip Phone was the rage.

Next were the flights. The destination was New Orleans, Louisiana (NOLA. Available seats? Zero. It's a small road block. Since there are no direct flights left we decide to look for Hubs where airlines home bases are. American Airlines home base is in Dallas, Texas. Delta's Hub is in Atlanta, Georgia. United is in Chicago and Southwest has a hub in Houston. Bingo! Houston is hot and steamy and a short ride to NOLA (New Orleans, Louisiana. Southwest Airlines runs a shuttle to New Orleans like the NYC Boston run every 90 minutes or so. Logistically, Houston would be choice number one and Dallas would be second. Direct flights to NOLA were over $800 round trip if they were available. I hit the phones. I reserve two to Houston round trip for around $300 each. Southwest was a no brainer at $200 round trip from Houston to NOLA.

Next decision? Who do I take? I have three brothers. First, I ask Doug as a courtesy. After all he took me 7 years earlier. He declines. Then I ask

Chris my brother who resides in Chicago. He has too much going on with his family and he can't make it. Lastly, I ask my older brother Greg as a formality. He always declines. I almost drop the phone when he accepts.

I call the airlines secure and pay for the tickets. One thing left lodging. I know NOLA has a lot of hotels, but everyone has been booked for 18 months for sure. I opt to secure a rental house or condo. I secure a two bedroom in the Irish Bayou. The owner swears it's a 20-minute ride to town. If we used the circles system on the map that we applied in Florida, we would be at least 2 circles out in radius. Not an optimal choice but at least it's a roof over our heads. There were no chains to implement the leap frog technique we utilized in Florida. This would require something clever. Back to the owner in the Irish Bayou. I sense he is lying about the distance and chew him down on price. I get the place for $700 for two nights. I figure once I have boots on the ground I can do some work and secure us a room one way or another. Apply what I have learned at the first Super Bowl and expand and figure out new methods.

We meet at Newark Airport and board a plane to Houston. It goes off without a hitch as all we have is small carry-ons. We hop the next shuttle out of Houston to NOLA and we barely have time for a drink before we land. We take a shuttle to the French Quarter. Once there we grab an infamous fried oyster Po'boy sub and an Ice-cold Dixie Beer. The place is jammed packed with fans and everyone is clearly ahead of us when it comes to drinks consumed. We walk outside, it's still daylight we pass several strip clubs then bar after crowded bar on Bourbon St. We come to a clearing by the court house and see the Café Dumunde on Decatur St. We consume the famous Chicory flavored coffee and hot beignets covered with powdered sugar. During the Civil War the Union Naval blockaded ports causing a coffee shortage. So, the locals mixed in chicory to make the coffee last longer. They serve it that way to this day on the banks of the Mississippi River.

We devise a plan to go to our rental house shower up then back into town to party. We hail a cab. My suspicions were correct, as it was further away than the owner had let on. I figured it was his way at getting back at a Yankee from up North. The house was completed gated. We had to go through locked gates and doors to enter. We weren't in the best of neighborhoods. We showered and went back into town it was an $80-dollar cab ride and took at least 45 minutes.

It was back to town where we found ourselves right smack in the middle of it. We ate dinner at some café then we stepped outside to smoke Cuban Cigars that I had bought. We saw a half a dozen fights and people being dragged off by the police and into the paddy wagon. We decided we had enough we bought some souvenirs and water then hailed a cab for the long ride home. When we arrived, we turned the AC full blast then wedged a chair against the door for added protection like you see in the movies.

Morning came fast, we showered and packed. I instructed Greg to bring his bag with us as we would get a room in town. He shot me a puzzled look. We packed and called a cab. We were there less than 24 hours we already spent $180 on cabs this wasn't going to work. The place was just a geographically undesirable shack on the Bayou. We never even saw the water! Time for plan B we had to adjust on the fly. Back in the French Quarter we canvassed other hotels. There was this tall high rise round Holiday Inn right on the riverbank. It was our 11Th hotel that we had checked. Smiling asking the craziest question…Do you have a room? Yes, we had one cancellation. Without asking price I said we'll take it. Lesson learned, persevere never be afraid to ask. Closer to game day there are always some cancellations or companies overbook and a few rooms slip through the cracks. Spontaneity got to love it! Leave no stone unturned. The room was expensive at $380 but the Superdome was a mile away!

It was time to shower get settled in and go out and have some fun and try to get a dinner reservation at Emeril's. He was the town's most famous new chef. Paul Prudhomme was the Godfather of NOLA chefs. Emeril was the young upstart. He was Portuguese by descent and hailed from Massachusetts. He worked at Commanders Palace the famed restaurant in the Garden District. You needed to wear a sport jacket to dine there. If I could eat at Emeril's that would make the trip complete. There was no way I could get in there it was booked solid a year in advance. We had heard that he opened a new restaurant with his disciples in the kitchen, it was called NOLA. We finally were able to eat at Nola's around 9:30. Boy was it worth the wait! It was now 20 hours until game time. With our tickets locked away in the hotel safe we decided to explore, we heard the Preservation Street Band play in an old Slave quarters. We wandered into a Voodoo store and bought a voodoo doll for my friend who was interviewing in Wall St.

I waited by the courthouse as my brother went to get pralines at the French Market. A young lady handed me a flier asking me to attend a party in the Warehouse district later that night. Her smile revealed fangs where her incisors were supposed to be. I wanted to believe she had them implanted. Who knows if they were real or not. I wasn't going to attend and be the main course to find out! It was about the time Ann Rice wrote the Vampire Diaries and they were in vogue. I discarded the flier in the trash bin and it was back to Bourbon St. for round two of the Debauchery.

On Bourbon St. the crowd was wilder on Saturday Night. Amongst the chaos, I met two girls and a guy that worked at Fox sports. I inquired as to where they were staying, and they gave me the name of their hotel. We still needed a room for after the game. Once we checked out Sunday morning we would attempt to get a room at this brand-new hotel. Hotel rooms can open on game day as a lot of people choose to leave especially if their team lost the Super Bowl. The wealthy Jet Setting Crowd are “Wheels Up” by midnight.

The next morning, we decided to have breakfast at “Mothers” on Poydras St. it was famous since 1938. The line wrapped around the building. We waited patiently to fill up our plates on the Buffett style serving line. Grits, Biscuits and Gravy, French Toast, Catfish, Eggs, Grilled Ham and Crawfish. We ate it all. Just before we entered the building we could see one of the teams boarding the bus to go to the Superdome. They were all dressed in suits wearing Head phones. We weren’t sure which squad it was, but I leaned towards the Packers. Parcells was known for keeping his team out of town for the big games to prevent distractions. By this time everywhere you looked there were Midwesterners wearing these obnoxious pie slice shaped plastic yellow cheese heads.

We walked towards the business district and checked on hotels as we passed by but to no avail. We finally arrived at the FOX Sports Hotel which was all a buzz. I walked over to the front desk and looked the young lady directly in the eyes. I explained that my cousin works for Fox and had informed me there were a few rooms left under their umbrella. Pure malarchy. She left the desk went into the office. She came out and confirmed they had just released two rooms for this evening. I threw my credit card down and politely stated we only needed one.

So, the Irish Bayou was a total bust. I ate the $600 loss at least we stayed there 1 night. Lesson learned. It was a mistake, cut your losses and move on. Now we could focus on game day. We swung by the Central Grocery and picked up two Muffuletta Sandwiches which weighed almost 3 Lbs. It's a round olive loaf focaccia. Inside it has Italian capicola, ham, cheese and olive oil. Then it was on towards the stadium. We stopped at various venues and bars along the way. The Budweiser wagon and Clydesdales horses were circling in this one parking lot and I nearly got run over trying to get in a picture with them.

The Superdome rose high into the sky like some alien Mother ship. It was truly immense! It is 273 feet high with a 680 ft diameter. It sits on 52 acres of land and has a 9-acre roof. Truly a sight to behold. It was 4:30 when we started going through checkpoints. Thank God we could bring the Muffulettas in. If they made use eat them outside, we would have missed the game. We arrived at our seats an hour before the game and got settled in. we were in the second level in the end zone in the 4th row from the rail. At least half of the game we would have excellent viewing. We were one of 76,468 people to witness the game live. T minus 1 hour till kick off Superbowl XXXI.

The Fox Network was broadcasting the Game with Pat Summerall and John Madden. I'm sure the Monticello Room back home was packed wall to wall. The teams ran from the tunnels as they were announced. Fireworks shot off making the field a cloudy mirage as the smoke lingered in the indoor arena. Then Luther Vandross walked out onto the field and rendered a soulful rendition of the Star-Spangled Banner. It never came close to Whitney's performance at my first Super Bowl. This is where things tend to pick up speed and can become a blur. Everything is timed to get in the multi-million dollar 30-second spots. The coin toss then the kick off then more fireworks. Both teams march up and down the field after the first quarter the underdog New England Patriots are leading 14-10.

During the Second Quarter the Green Bay Packers explode with 17 points while holding the Patriots to zero. Bret Favre completed an 81-yard pass and ran one in from the 2-yard line. Add a field goal and the Patriots were in shock.

Halftime seemed to take forever. It was the Blues Brothers with Dan Ackroyd, James Brown and ZZ Top. We didn't really care who won. Parcells was a great coach, he signed Dave Meggitt from the Giants and Curtis Martin from the NY Jets on his squad to accompany QB Drew Bledsoe. But they had an uphill battle against Sack leader Reggie White who registered 3 sacks. Midway through the quarter Curtis Martin scored from 18 yards out to close the gap to 27-21. Up until now it was a great game.

During the ensuing kickoff, The Packers' Desmond Howard ran 99 yards back to score a Touchdown. This deflated the sails of the New England Patriots and they didn't score again. The final score was Green Bay Packers 35 and New England Patriots 21. We watched the celebration and were happy to see the legendary Green Bay Packers back on top of the NFL once more as they paraded the Lombardi Trophy around the field.

Ironically, when I returned home I came to find out that Vince Lombardi was laid to rest in a Mount Olivet Cemetery right up the road in Middletown NJ. He never had a losing season and died of cancer at age 57.

My Brother Greg & I at Super Bowl XXXI

New Orleans 1997

Chapter 9

Life Is What Happens When You Plan…

The years start to slide by. You get married, have kids it all begins to blend together. Time waits for no man! You work like a dog you try to relax on vacations. You barely have time for yourself. You go from being number one, to the person that pays the bills, walks the dog and takes out the garbage. Life becomes a routine of endless mundane tasks. All I ever asked for was a little appreciation. Kids come first you're always last. Life becomes very real. You find yourself sacrificing for everyone else. You must keep moving forward. Now all the expendable cash has other outlets Preschool, nannies, beach clubs, gymnastics then private schools. Your waistline becomes bigger your hair more grey. If you're lucky you have golf or a boat as an outlet. You sleep 5 maybe 6 hours. If you manage to get through this phase alive, there's hope. Then there's Little League or coaching kids in several sports. All the while they want the newest gadget. I had two children I forbid video games and cell phones until they were 10. They grew up on three acres by the beach I wanted them outside, not trapped behind a computer screen or a phone like the walking zombies you see today. To some extent I was successful. It's an extremely hard job being a parent especially if you attempt to be hands-on and do it correctly.

It was 2001, I was working for Goldman Sachs at 1 NY Plaza at the lower tip of Manhattan. The Summer was over, and I was putting in 12-hour days as usual. The only good thing about Summer ending, is that Football season begins. I think without Football there would be more people being diagnosed with depression. My daughter was turning 3 on September 16th and I was planning her Birthday. We already had the pony rides, pig roast and lobster fest. It was September 11th, it was a beautiful sunny Tuesday, not a cloud in the sky. I was sitting in my Aeron chair on Goldman Sachs main Trading Desk. I had just got off the phone with Tuck he was loving the fact that I was now married with kids as well and had limited time to do anything fun. He had been Tuna fishing in the Canyons 100 miles off the NJ Coast on Monday. I asked if he caught any fish? He replied: yes, and to call Kenny Jags as he had the Tuna. Unfortunately, he had thrown his back out on the trip. It was the usual trader short sound bite conversation. I replied: Ok jackass and hung up. It was 8:25. My desk was on the 50th or top floor. It had a full view of the down town skyline. My friend Holly, an assistant to my boss, asked me to go to the cafeteria. That was on the 43th floor. She was a petite girl from London fully equipped with the accent and the British sarcasm that I grew to love. I looked out over the harbor and pointed to the ferry I took in every day. She's said big deal lets discuss bonuses as

Goldman Sachs fiscal year ends in November. We were facing Southeast. It was then I noticed paper floating around the building from the northwest. The only time this ever occurred was during a ticker tape parade. There was nothing scheduled. I began to see some black smoke and realized something wasn't quite right. We walked out of the cafeteria at a quickened pace. Along the way we encountered a runner or bike messenger he was frantic. He said he saw a plane hit the World Trade Center. I inquired, a Cessna or passenger plane? He said he didn't know but it was big there was a hole in building. It was then I realized this wasn't any accident. This was terrorism and we were under attack.

We ran to the elevator bank and pressed the up button. At my desk, I had a clear view of the towers I wanted to see and access the situation. We entered the elevator and pressed 50. The doors opened on the 47th floor we saw people running around chaotically. It was the beginning of the panic. There was a managing director of mine yelling and jumping both feet off the ground. We are under attack a Russian MIG just shot missiles at the World Trade Center. I said WTF is he talking about? Just then the elevators closed, and we were summoned to the lobby. All elevators were called to the lobby and shut down as the safety procedures require. Everyone else on my desk would have to walk down 50 flights.

By the time we ran out of the building we could see massive smoke billowing out of the World Trade Center as a second plane hit the other tower. Phones didn't work and there was plenty of disinformation. It was sheer panic. I took Holly by the hand and we ran into Battery Park which abutted the Hudson River. I wasn't sure who or why we were being attacked. I knew we would be safe from falling debris as we were far enough away from any tall buildings. By now it was pure chaos. The roads were filled with emergency vehicles. The smoke was getting worse. As word spread more ferries came to rescue people off the Island of Manhattan. I begged Holly to get on the Ferry with me, but she was worried about her beloved beagle Sophie. I made her promise not to take any subways but to walk up the FDR Drive. She agreed, and we parted ways. I made it on the third ferry out. By this time the word of a terror attack was spreading. The captain made everyone spread out as the boat was listing to one side. As we backed away from the dock you could hear sirens from the emergency vehicles rushing towards the scene.

We cleared Governors Island and you could see that both towers were engulfed in flames. News was spreading that it was terrorists that hijacked passenger aircraft and purposefully flew them into the towers. I said to Kenny a friend from HS that was standing next to me at least they didn't knock them down. Just then in slow motion like a kid's erector set toy, Tower 1 started crumble in slow motion. I teared up. I was shaking. A man next to me dropped to his knees and started praying from a Bible he was carrying. Girls were crying and shouting in disbelief. The TV above the bar broadcast that the Pentagon was attacked and President Bush was already up in Air force One. The breaking news lines scrolled across that all planes were ordered to be grounded or they would be shot down. When I got off the boat I was still having issues processing what I had just experienced. My wife was there with my 1-year old son. I said let's go to the bank take out $10,000 cash and go get my daughter Ally and drive out into the country.

I arrived home only to watch more chaos unfold on the television set as the second tower collapsed. My brother Greg takes the NJ Path Train through there around that time every morning we were feverishly trying to reach him. It was hours before we located him in Brooklyn at least we were both unscathed. Then I thought of Tuck and his crew at Cantor Fitzgerald. He had been a great friend who was always there to help. What could I do? Was there any way I could help? I was just on the phone with him 15 minutes prior to the attack. I felt utterly helpless. How do you process this?

There were memorials and funerals for months it was one of the hardest periods of all our lives.

Things would never really be normal again for all these families. Wall St was never the same after that.

I remembered the conversations I had with Tuck, all the people he introduced me to. The fun times at the Wall St events. I will never forget his razor-sharp wit and his generosity. I had other friends TJ and Craig who golfed that day and were spared. The few people that survived that disaster had to deal with survivor guilt. They set up charities to support their friend's families. They may be gone but they will never be forgotten.

I tried to make something positive out of this horrific event. I promised myself to live everyday as if it's your last. As you get older you realize, life isn't a dress rehearsal. Try to be kind and helpful to those around you.

I recalled that years earlier, before I was even married, Tuck made me promise that if I ever had a son to send him to his Alma Mater Christian Brothers Academy CBA. I honored that promise. My son Stephen graduated CBA class of 2018.

Chapter 10 Ticket Prices Plunge

After battling to deal with what occurred on 9/11 I managed to get out of that high-rise office building any chance I could. I would go out for an hour lunch which was unheard of at Goldman Sachs. I along with others weren't too fond of being 50 floors up in the air as a sitting duck target. As time went by these fears subside. It was January 2002, the week before the Super Bowl and I received a phone from an old Floor Clerk Dominic who was now working at JP Morgan, if my memory serves me correctly. He asked if I wanted two tickets to the Super Bowl which was in 5 days. He explained that certain customers were afraid to go as they thought terrorists would blow the place up. I was glad to hear from him he was like my kid brother. Early in his career I protected him from a managing partner perhaps this was payback.

I wasn't sure what to say at first, but some words blurted out. I asked where the seats were. He said they were good 9th row on the 20 Yard line. I thought maybe this is just what I need to get me out of my funk. It was in New Orleans, so I knew the lay of the land. Why not go and try to feel alive once again? I told him yes and he agreed to sell them to me at cost. Face value of tickets were now $400. I had been to the Show twice before and thoroughly enjoyed it. I had never sat in the 9th row. Finally, something to look forward to. I went home that night and pondered who do I bring?

Once again, step Number One.... I had the coveted tickets. Next, who was I going to take? I called Brother Chris in Chicago and he balked. I'm not even sure what his excuse was this time. So then standard protocol. I call my brother Doug and get right to the point. You took me to my first Super Bowl would you like to go to see the St Louis Rams against the New England Patriots in New Orleans ? He declines. Then there's brother Greg. I call him up hey you want to go to the Show again? He declines as he is too busy with work. Do these guys realize how difficult it is to get your hands-on tickets?

After 9/11 I realized how fleeting life can be and that the most valuable commodity isn't money, diamonds or Gold its time! We only have a finite amount of it. Life is short! I lost a lot of Friends way before their time. Live your life as if every day's your last! Carpe Diem... seize the day make the best out of things. We are only here for a short time.

Now I had never gone past the list of brothers. So, there I was on the B-team list, the second string, list of friends. I called Dave a college buddy in California. I could barely get the words out when he yelled I'm in! Well that's more like it. I tell him I have the tickets the and to get his ass to NOLA by Saturday and work on hotel rooms. He calls back two hours later. He informs me that he secured his airline tickets and a lead on a room. His Girlfriend work in Hospitality services at a prominent hotel in California. She has a buddy who is a manager at the hotel connected to the Superdome. She contacts him and calls in a favor. Just like that we have a room for two days in a hotel connected to the Superdome stadium! Boy this is getting easier. It's my 3rd Super Bowl, I practically had to do nothing except book airline tickets.

Remember what I said earlier be open to meeting new people and keep in touch with people from the past. Once you get the tickets the rest falls into place. The resources in the larger cities present plenty of opportunities for lodging and great restaurants.

So, I arrive early Saturday in Houston once again and take the Southwest Shuttle I meet Dave and we head over to the Hyatt to secure the room and get the layout. Security will be tighter than it was in Tampa for Super Bowl XXV. We score dinner reservations at NOLA. We had tickets, we had the closest room connected to the stadium. This would allow us to go directly through the underground Mall and alleviate a lot of the pre-security checkpoints. The only issue is trying not to have a hangover for gameday. We shower up hit the town we eat dinner at a new place called Fish. Sitting at the table across from us is the Rams Quarterback Kurt Warner's wife. The place is huge and noisy, and the food is great. Everything here is spread out it's hard to recognize former players.

The NFL and sponsors throw private parties where they attend. The most sought-after party is the MAXIM Party. So, we make the best of it and decide to head over to the Riverboat Casino to play some cards. They ask you for $10-dollar cover to get in. I stop dead in my tracks, I refuse to pay a cover to gamble. I explain that in New Jersey they give you a free bus ride and a $10-dollar roll of quarters to lure you into losing more money. It falls on deaf ears and we retreat into the soupy night air. It's been extremely humid since we arrived. The Alcohol consumption just acerbates it. We circle back into town and grab a few drinks listen to jazz and are entertained by the girls showing their boobs for cheap plastic beads. It was Mardi Gras on steroids! Around 1 am we stumble back to the room hydrate and sleep until noon .

The next day we have breakfast sent up from room service. I plan to meet Dominic and exchange $800 for the two tickets. I walk to his hotel and I get cash from an ATM. While making the exchange a guy comes up to me and gives me my bank card that I left in the machine. In NY, that never would have happened. It would have been maxed out on airline tickets or clothes from some department store. I guess I was in a bit of a rush to carelessly leave my card in the ATM slot. We stroll into a bar and have a cocktail as we haven't seen each other in a couple of years. We agree to meet at Halftime as our seats were close and we would grab dinner after the game.

Dave and I decide to go to Central Grocery in the French Market and pick up Muffulettas. On the way we stop at one of the oldest restaurants in New Orleans adjacent to the Court House. They have this huge caldron in the window which opens onto the front sidewalk. The pungent smell of Old Bay seasonings wafts down the alley. In the huge hanging pot steam rises above Crawfish Boil. We saunter in order two orders of Crawdaddies. They have been cooking them in this fashion for over 200 years. The waitress glides across the well-worn wooden floor to bring us over two Ice cold Dixie beers. We devour the food and our mouths are burning from the spices. It's now 4 hours before game time. We meander about the French Quarter where you could feel the energy building. Parades, Floats, people in costumes and the glaring sounds of slide trombones and tubas reverberate from the back alleys. Vintage NOLA!

The Super Bowl was a week later this year, it's February 3rd as the players had a two-week layoff from their Championship games. It's now 4 hours prior to kickoff. We pick up some souvenirs and slowly walk back towards the hotel. The Security was already amped up. Cars were not allowed within a mile of the Superdome. Everyone was on foot. You could feel the police presence. Heavily Armored vehicles were everywhere. All night long you could hear Air force Fighter Jets flying overhead. Ex-President, George W Bush was set to do the coin flip. It was his way to assist in calming the spooked fans. Back at the hotel we got organized and scoped out the route that we had to take to enter the stadium. The Hotel was above a shopping mall which was connected to the Superdome. The place was crawling with Police and Sheriffs from every county and parish in Louisiana.

There were bomb sniffing dogs and National Guardsman as well. I believed it was the safest place in the country that day. Terrorists rely on the element of surprise. Trying to do something in this well guarded fortress would be both foolish and ineffective.

Back at the room we get organized and hydrated. With two and a half hours to go we descend into the lower level. In the mall there's about 300 people funneling into the one entrance they have into the Stadium. It's very orderly, within a half an hour they are scanning our tickets and we are within the confines of the Superdome. The excitement builds. The Halftime show is U2 and they will be doing something special to honor the 9-11 victims and heroes. It's 5:00 PM, 90 minutes until kickoff. We see the huge lines of people attempting to enter. We encounter scalpers as there were plenty of extra tickets. I thought I was hearing things when he said $250 a ticket. He was selling them $150 cheaper than the $400-dollar face value. I guess there were many fans that decided it wasn't worth the risk. I was a Wall St. analyst who was several blocks from Ground Zero when it happened. As an Eye witness I would not be deterred. I would not let them win. By being afraid you let the terrorists win. By the time we entered the stadium tickets dropped to $100 a piece. I recall after the first Super Bowl in Tampa fans were offering $100 just for the stub as it was the first ticket to have a hologram on it. Now ticket prices plummeted. Supply was greater than demand for the first time in modern day Super Bowl History.

Super Bowl Ticket distribution by the NFL is broken down as follows: The hosting team receives 5% of the tickets available. Then the AFC and NFC champions each receive 17.5%. That takes care of 40%. The other 29 teams share in 34.8% while the NFL keeps the remaining 25.2%. So, the true fan base only receives an opportunity to fill up 1/3 of the stadium unless they buy tickets from a source other than their teams' lottery.

The NFL distributes tickets to Refs and Executives. Then their sponsors share in the rest according to what they spend. This breakdown indicates how difficult it is to acquire tickets. It also indicates where to look to secure tickets in an unconventional way.

We slowly enter the stadium to scout out are seats. The fans are amped up. It's Super Bowl XXXVI the Saint Louis Rams against the New England Patriots. Bill Parcells' Patriots had lost the Super Bowl to the Packers 5 years earlier.

Bill Belichick was the defensive Coordinator with the Giants and the Patriots. He was now the Head Coach of the Patriots as Bill Parcells went to my NY Jets and lost in the Championship game with them.

There are 73,000 fans in attendance We find our section and walk down to row 9. Something wasn't right Row 9 was the first row. We asked the usher he affirmed we were in the right seats. I was flabbergasted. You mean to tell me I'm sitting in the first row at the Super Bowl? Once again, I'm in a bit of shock. We shake hands with or neighboring seat holders who were sitting with two buxom younger ladies. We grab drinks and I lean over the wall. We are on the 20 Yard line I'm so close to the field I can't believe it. We talk to the cameramen and the cheerleaders. Then we see Mariah Carey come out of the tunnel on out left to sing the National Anthem. We stand and the crowd shouts USA when she culminates. You could feel the hair stand up on the back of your neck as fireworks explode. George W does the coin toss and again everything starts to speed up.

The kickoff ensues the Rams score a field goal on their first possession. They had an explosive offense nicknamed "The Greatest Show on Turf" . But the defensive mastermind Bill Belichick had other ideas. By halftime, the underdog New England Patriots capitalized on two turnovers were up 14-3.

Mike Martz was the head coach of the Rams. He was faced with the arduous task of reprogramming his team to claw back in the 2nd half.

Finally, halftime, our seat neighbors ran to the bathroom with their Buxom Blondes in tow they promised to bring back a couple of cocktails. Right below us was Bono he was waiting for the ground crew to assemble the stage. We yelled, and he waved back, we took pics as they ran onto the field he performed some of his more notable hits before going into the ballad " Where the streets have no name "as they scrolled the names of the fallen 9-11 victims and heroes on this giant screen suspended from the Superdome roof. It was surreal. Bono an Irish man was wrapped in an American Flag. I read at least 20 names of people I knew as they scrolled upwards to the sky. But the one that stood out was Michael Tucker. I'm not sure if he ever had a chance to get to a Super Bowl but he was a diehard Giants fan. I had come here to escape but there was his name and a dozen other acquaintances. It was a powerful display. I think if he was still here he probably would have been at that game. I sank back in my chair and was glad that the World could read the names of all these innocent people. They were guilty of nothing they just showed up for work on time. I was in a bit of a trance when I felt a cold sensation on my hand and it was the drinks our seatmates had promised.

The stadium was full of people with mixed emotions when the second half commenced. This was a prime example of how we use Sports or Entertainment of a form of escapism. The stadium began to rock as the second half got under way. The Patriots scored quickly to make it 17-3. The Rams hadn't scored since the first quarter. This finally changed as Kurt Warner led his team up and down the field in the 4th Quarter to tie the game at 17 apiece. John Madden and Pat Summerall were the Broadcasters. I watched the replays after the game and Madden was suggesting the Patriots go for the tie as they were backed up by their own end zone with the clock running out.

Tom Brady a 2nd year Quarterback out of Michigan had replaced Bledsoe earlier in the season. He had 1:30 minutes left and no timeouts. Veteran Super Bowl winning quarterback Kurt Warner had just thrown a 28-yd Touchdown pass to tie the game at 17-17.

The game began to go into warp speed. One minute the Patriots were right in front of me the next minute they were crossing 50-yard line. I struggled to get up out of my seat as the drinks had taken their effect. The whole stadium was yelling and cheering. Could they engineer a walk off field goal as the Giants did at my first Super Bowl? Belichick's Offensive Coordinator was Charlie Weiss they decided to go for it. Brady initially threw 3 passes to his running back J R Redmond who quickly stepped out of bounds Then with a surgeon's precision he methodically threw passes in front of the coverage and the receivers stepped out of bounds stopping the game clock. The clock ticked away 20-19-18 The place was a mad house. You could barely hear the person next to you. One more completion to the 31. Time stops for no man 10-9-8....Brady spikes the Ball. I look up at the clock it says .07 just 7 seconds left.

General Belichick yells for the Field Goal team to take the field. Adam Vinatieri lines up the kick the game goes into slow motion compared to the frenetic pace of the last 1:23 minutes. I stretch out over the rail to get a good view of the kick at the far end of the field. The snap is good the Rams defense extends upward to block it. Vinatieri takes his two and a half steps and powers the ball through the uprights. The clock strikes zero! The crowd erupts! Fireworks explode! Confetti and balloons are everywhere. The sound is deafening! The underdog New England Patriots pull off a startling defeat of the Champion St Louis Rams with a walk off Field Goal 20-17. After several high fives I sink back into my number 9 first-row seat and shake my head. I sit there in disbelief. Once again, I am fortunate enough to witness a last-minute upset win at the Super Bowl. This is the pure beauty that sports can portray. It is Grand Theatre when the outcome isn't known until the final whistle.

Chapter 11 Every Dog Has It's Day!

The celebration continued. We watched as players, coaches and their family members passed around the Lombardi trophy. The stadium was one third full as crazed fans from Boston relished their first Super Bowl win. Bill Belichick finally was in the right place again. After winning two Super Bowls with the Giants he had a brief stint with the Cleveland Browns where he was fired in 1995. He later rejoined Parcels with the Patriots and then the NY Jets. I recall the bizarre press conference where Parcells retired from being Head coach of the NY Jets. They named Bill Belichick Head Coach and he refused to take the job. It wasn't bad enough that the NY Jets screwed things up on the field now they couldn't even get the press conferences right.

After that bizarre NY Jets debacle, Belichick took the head job at the New England Patriots. They had a new owner Robert Kraft they redesigned the uniforms to resemble a super hero the rest as they say is history. Here in New England he was the Head Coach and he finally received the credit he was due.

Outside was pure pandemonium. We made our way to the French Quarter and somehow got into NOLA and ate dinner around 11 PM. We partied a bit then stumbled back into our hotel. What a game!

The next morning, I called home to see how my parents enjoyed the game at their new retirement community they had moved into. They said it wasn't the same without all the boys in that packed *Monticello Room*. I promised next year I'd come over cook up wings and dinner and set up the box pools. I told them all about the events that had unfolded they got a kick out of the stories and enjoy living vicariously through my adventures.

We went to the airport and I bid my farewell to my College buddy Dave who was still sky high from his first Super Bowl. As I sat there in the terminal I tried to decompress as I was headed back into reality. The 60-hour work weeks and the repercussions from 9-11 on the Financial Markets and everyday life. On the plane ride home, I replayed the events of the last 72 hours. The adrenaline rush of getting here, the festive atmosphere, the enormity of the Game itself. I wished everyone could experience this thrill, but it's only limited to 80,000 or so fortunate people. I had been to my 3rd Super Bowl and it was Epic! My entire life I had just wanted to "GET TO THE SHOW" just once. Now I' m catching up to Brooklyn Al. What if I could share my stories with others or better yet tell people how to get to the Show?

Chapter 12 Pre-Gaming in Miami

Once again, the years start to fly by. I left Goldman Sachs and joined a small boutique firm, Rochdale Securities. I still commuted on the Sea Streak Ferry, but it wasn't much fun after 9-11. It had become all business. I negotiated a deal to work from, New Jersey so I could alleviate the 2Hour travel time and spend more time with my children. I could work from home on Friday's and drive them back and forth to school. I would always be there to participate in school events. Business was great as we successfully navigated the Housing & Financial Collapse of 2008. I had a large fund overseas that I was doing business with daily. Their head trader frequented Miami often and I'd fly down to meet him.

It was 2010, when he informed me he was coming into Miami for the Super Bowl. It wasn't until the week before the game that he suggested I'd secure tickets. It had been 8 years since my previous Super Bowl and prices had sky rocketed. It would be my second Super Bowl in Florida but the first in Miami. I booked airfare to Ft. Lauderdale on Continental Airlines. I arrived at Newark Airport two hours early. It was a Thursday and I whizzed through the TSA line.

I had plenty of time to spare so I ducked into Gallagher's Steak Restaurant which was brand new in the terminal. I hopped up onto a barstool and ordered a cocktail. I recognized a guy from the gym across the bar and waved. I yelled across where are you going? He said Miami. I asked are you going to the Game? Again, he affirmed.

I picked up my carry-on bag and moved closer. I had time to kill I might as well hear about his journey to the SHOW. We ordered steaks and I asked him how he acquired his tickets. He explained that he was doing a friend a favor who owns a Specialized Travel Company. He said they put All inclusive packages together for Football Games and Private Concerts. He continued to explain, that there are a lot of players who don't want to attend unless they are playing in the game. He reached into his jacket pocket and pulled out a thick stack of Super Bowl tickets. My eyes grew larger than the coffee saucers on the counter. It was if I had seen a ghost! ***JESUS HOW MANY TICKETS IN THAT STACK?*** He said they had 70 customers or so going to the game. I had never seen that many Super Bowl Tickets at one time. How much was the Package? I believe he said $8500 which included Hotel, Ticket, Airfare and Meals. Do you have any extras as I still needed two tickets to the game? He replied: that he would ask his buddy when he arrived in Miami. This would be the first time I was going to the Big Game without tickets in hand. I had called several scalpers, but they were all very expensive. I choose to wait until I arrived in Miami as the two teams that were playing weren't big city draws. It was Super Bowl XLIV the New Orleans Saints against the Indianapolis Colts. I figured it was a calculated risk. The last Super Bowl I attended the tickets plunged 70% just prior to game time. There was a good chance that even the price of the scalper's tickets would drift lower. The Colts had already won a Super Bowl, but the New Orleans Saints hadn't. The Demand would be greater with the Saints fans for that very reason. I was gambling that these fans didn't have as deep pockets as the larger fan bases did.

I asked my new friend where he was staying? He responded: The Fontainebleau. He said the owner of the company's father was close with Sinatra and they would go there back in the heyday. He wanted to stay there for nostalgic reasons. Just then the bartender interrupted. Can I get you gentleman anything else? We both replied just the check. We shook hands and exchanged numbers before heading towards the boarding gate.

Miami was slowly starting to turn as the economy was bottoming. When I was there in 2008 there were real estate brokers and salespeople begging you to come in and see condos. It was very depressing. They had over built on speculation and prices had plunged. You couldn't walk down the sidewalk without getting hawked or accosted. Million Dollar Condos were going for $300,000. There was South American and European buyers snapping up the steep discounts. The US Dollar was weak, and this currency fluctuation was in their favor. Those who were brave enough to snap up properties were rewarded with double and in some cases triple returns on their investment a decade later.

The Infamous Fontainebleau Hotel had just reopened after undergoing a Billion Dollar renovation. The place had seven pools, hundreds of hotel rooms as well as condos. It was a favorite of the Rat Pack in the 50's and 60's. In Florida, there were thousands of hotels to choose from so lodging wouldn't be an issue. Flights to Florida were also easy you had your choice of several airports. Miami, Ft Lauderdale or West Palm were all convenient to Sun Stadium.

I had booked a room at the Gansevoort South. This was a high-rise hotel right on the Beach located in the Northern section of South Beach. In the lobby they had a 150-foot long Shark Tank. The place was gorgeous. I had booked a condo that was attached to the Hotel. The Roof Top bar was spectacular. It had views of the Ocean and Downtown Miami. They played that rhythmic spa-like beat of Miami, it was so relaxing. I had a cabana poolside where gorgeous waitresses brought over frozen drinks and overpriced Latin-style food. No one seemed to care about the inflated prices. It was 75 degrees and I was getting a tan on a rooftop and sipping Mojitos in January while it snowed back home. It doesn't get much better than this.

It was the end of January and I had turned Bearish on stocks the market had become a bit overbought. My client didn't agree with me and still decided to hold onto his long positions. The market tanked. This was the one thing that was disrupting this surreal scene. After 25 years on Wall St. I realized it's better to go away with zero positions if you can. Fund Managers aren't afforded this luxury, but they still can hedge and protect their investments in case of a sudden down draft. Trading is an extremely stressful occupation, you need to get away relax and recharge. If you don't you will end up making the wrong decisions. It's kind of like "Murphy's Law" If anything can go wrong it probably will. Over the next two days of the weeks the losses mounted. This ruined the whole experience for him and put a damper on it for me.

My customer flew in from overseas and we met at the W Hotel for a cocktail. The place was crawling with celebrities and Sports Stars. We decided to go to NOBU to get Sushi which was in the back of the famed Shore Club. After dinner it was back to the Fontainebleau the place was bustling. I saw Dan Marino I over by the bar holding court all dapper and tan. I believe there was an ESPN party out along the Beach. I didn't have tickets to this event and there was no way to get in as security was iron clad. I sat in the lobby and people watched as my customer retired to his room.

I met one of my best Friend's son who played Quarterback at Notre Dame and Indiana. I knew him since he was 8 years old. His dad Larry was also diehard Jets fan. We would go to Giants Stadium as he had 5 tickets in the end zone. I watched him grow up. Years later, I would take my 8-year old son to the Jet's game. We all sat together. I turned to my son he smiled as it was his first game. I leaned over and said you now have the Jets Curse. He asked does it hurt. I laughed and said sometimes. I assured him not to worry as everyone in the stadium has it. You see we haven't been to a Superbowl since I was your age. We laughed and went onto enjoy the game as a fathers and sons often do.

I met Larry's son Matt and his sister in the crowded lobby and we had a cocktail and I told him that I had a Buddy from Goldman Sachs who played at Univ of Indiana and with the NY Jets. We caught up on old times and I told him stories about his Father and our days on Wall St. together.

After they left I heard some guy singing Sinatra. He was about my age and bald sitting at his table was an older gentleman who turned out to be his father. Then I spotted my new friend from Newark Airport with the tickets. We sat down had a couple of drinks and his father told stories about Sinatra in the old days. After an hour or so he got up to bring his elderly Father back to the room and asked me to stay in the lobby. It was about 11pm or so the place was bustling.

There was a huge line to get in their brand-new night club called LIVE. Again, the Velvet Ropes! I walked about the grand Lobby and I ran into the "BUS" Jerome Bettis the Hall of Fame running back for the Pittsburgh Steelers. He was holding court telling fans stories. He was in sweats and still looked like he could run you over. He was the nicest guy taking pictures and laughing. A true ambassador of the game.

Then Daymond John walked by me. I had recognized him from the pilot of Shark Tank the previous Summer. I yelled FUBU twice the acronym for his clothing line For Us by US, but he failed to turn around. It wasn't until I yelled Shark Tank that he turned and headed my direction. He had a huge guy with him either a buddy or a body guard. We talked about Shark Tank and how I had been on CNBC for years. I told him I thought it would be a hit and that he was doing a great job. I also asked why is that guy Kevin so annoying. He laughed and walked away melting into what had become a sea of people.

Just then my friend returned after putting his Dad to bed. He asked if I wanted to go into club LIVE. I gave a nod yes. I didn't let on with an inquisitive look as most would when faced with such an impossible task. I walked to the front of the line where "DR J" Julius Erving was arguing with the bouncer to get inside. Either the bouncer didn't recognize one of the most famous basketball players and the father of the Dunk or his name wasn't on the list. My new-found buddy said a few words to the bouncer he glanced at his clipboard and we walked right through ahead of at least 200 *wannabee* patrons.

Inside the place was cavernous. A huge rectangle dance floor with a 5-story ceiling with strobe lights and mirrors glittering everywhere. There was an upstairs, where people could look over the chaos below. The bathrooms were located up there as well. The bar was located along the entire right wall. The place was an enormous madhouse. I bought a round of drinks then made my way to the upstairs bathroom. On the way out of the bathroom I ran into a Hedge Fund Manager who I knew from back in NYC. We exchanged numbers and told me he had rented a yacht for a week. He invited me to his table. We made our way through the gyrating bodies on the dance floor. We arrived at his spot comprised of three tables which were graced with of the largest bottles of Champagne and Vodka I had ever seen. Girls danced around to the hypnotic beat spun out by the DJ whose booth was adjacent to us. It was pure mayhem . It was studio 54 on steroids. We partied until 4:30 until I stumbled out and took a cab back to my hotel. After all, this was only Thursday Night. I had to pace myself as I learned from previous Super Bowls. The bill was over $12,000. Thank God I was a guest.

Chapter 13 It's Your Lucky day…

It was Friday morning and the Markets tumbled again. My customer was miserable. He was with a couple of other big Bank Brokers when he arrived at my Roof Top pool. I ordered a bucket of beer and a bottle of Vodka they all settled in. The guy had bad anxiety over the markets they all left with barely drinking. I told him I was staying, and I'd catch up later. There were plenty of thirsty people around the pool that didn't want to pay 12 bucks for a cocktail yet had an enormous appetite for free drinks. I'm always amused by how popular you become when ordering bottle service. Once that bottle is empty the crowd scatters and it's you and the check.

As the sun started to go over the building it was nearing 5 O'clock. Time to shower get ready for dinner wherever that may be. We decided to go to Joes Stone Crab house. This place has been here for 100-years and is a Florida institution. They made stone crabs so popular that the fisherman who trap them are only allowed to take one claw off and through the crab back in the bay to regenerate another one during the next molt. The place was originally a shack in 1913 that had now grown into a block long restaurant with a large takeout area on Washington St. Back then you would get 3 or 4 whole crabs for .75 cents now its $90 dollars for 5 jumbo claws. They vertically integrated by buying their own traps and boats. It's located at the Southern tip of South Beach, in the 1980's it was surrounded by crack houses and run-down garden apartments. Now there were cranes everywhere building 40 floor high rises with apartments that sell well into the millions.

I saw the Maitre'd slipped him $25 bucks and he put our names in the book smiled at me and said two hours. It was as if I insulted him with a measly $25 bucks. The place was jam packed it was Super Bowl weekend. I'm on my second scotch when in walk the Manning Brothers. Football Quarterback Royalty one taller than the other. There was ELI QB for the NY Giants his father Archie former QB of the New Orleans Saints and the oldest brother Cooper who was injured and never played in the NFL. The most famous brother was Peyton Manning who was playing in his 2nd Super Bowl that weekend. They walked right in and were seated immediately. An hour and 45-minutes later they seated us at a cramped table by the Bar. We ordered Jumbo crab claws, Cold Beer and key lime pie. When in Rome do as the Romans. It was worth the wait as always.

It was 10 O'clock we got dropped off at some Hotel that was hosting the MAXIM party on the Beach. Again, security at these extravagant and over-subscribed parties was over the top. My customer has two tickets and he decided to take his brother into the party. He says once inside he will scout for a ticket and get myself and his two other friends inside. I could care less actually but wait patiently outside. I realize I'm standing Right next to Mark Sanchez the Jets QB and his 8-man crew. I tap him on the shoulder and explain I've been a NY Jet fan longer than he was alive! Instead of waiting to get into this party you should be playing in the game. I said how could you lose that championship game? You guys had the Colts beat. He shrugs and says next year as his eyes turn towards the gorgeous scantily clothed Maxim models strutting by. His entourage walks briskly behind him as they get whisked inside. We are still outside the velvet ropes, a clearly defined line in the sand separating the A-listers from the wannabees. I never had the patience for this type of exclusionary bullcrap. I must admit it was amusing people watching. Another person walks out, and I recognize him as Billionaire John Paul Dejoria with his wife. He co-founded John Paul Mitchell Systems with hairdresser Paul Mitchell. He also co-founded Patron Tequila.

After an hour wait they come back and said no other tickets. Prudently, I walk back to my hotel as its nearing 1 AM. I enter the lobby and see Chris Rock heading towards the elevator. I yell out . Yo Chris Rock you sucked on Saturday Night Live, but you are one funny bastard now. He smiles and waves as he enters the awaiting elevator.

I head to bed and realize I have a day and a half to acquire tickets to the game. The next morning, I call the scalper who still has tickets and he still wants $4500. The seats are in the Saints endzone in the 25th row we settle on a price of

$4200 and we agree to meet and exchange payment. It's Saturday, I have the tickets and we go to the Sushi bar to eat lunch. I run into the Hedge Fund Manager and he invites me to his yacht. I inform him I'll call him later if I can make it as I got a rogue trader who has taken a beating over the past week.

I head back to my pool to relax my customer meets me there and says he thinks he must fly back early to Europe. He is afraid he will get fired after losing a substantial amount of money over the past week while he is in Miami partying. I'm livid. I just purchased the tickets. You couldn't have told me on Friday! Then he asks me to take his friend instead. I said what? Now I'm rally pissed its 24 hours till kick off. I paid a lot of money for these seats. I'll fly someone down or take one of the girls I met back at the hotel. He is adamant that's his condition. On Wall St. you learn quickly that loyalty is expected and usually rewarded. I had a valid argument, but which decision would affect my bottom line?

He goes back to his hotel and books the next plane back to Europe. Now I am forced entertain his child hood friend who happens to be out of work at the time. A tall, thin, red headed Irish kid from Long Island. Usually when people are out of work they are humble. Not this kid, he still had a chip on his shoulder. I always felt respect is something you earn not expect. He was a bit of a wiseass who lived vicariously through his successful buddies. At least this was the vibe I was picked up on. How lucky was he? I don't think there was another out of work fan at that Super Bowl. This broke mother 'effer was going to the Super Bowl on my dime.

This wasn't what I had planned out. It wasn't even in the realm of probabilities that I could fathom. If only my customer had listened. He could have hedged or cut his long exposure he could have attended the game. In Either case, what's done is done. I'd have to make the best of it. It is what it is.

My customer leaves, I eat dinner at a Cuban place then head to the Fontainebleau. I run into my buddy who owns the specialized Travel Company we drink and sing Sinatra. Then he informs me he is taking another group of people on a charted jet to Hawaii to see Bon Jovi play and he won't be attending the game. Unfortunately, he didn't have any extra tickets. There weren't that many people excited about the Big Game this year except the New Orleans fans. They were hungry for a victory and they sure new how-to party. I decided to go to bed, wake up, hit the gym and have a nice breakfast then get to the stadium early and there are Saints fans everywhere!

Chapter 14 Caveat Emptor!!! Buyer Beware

I woke up a little later than expected as I had the Blackout Shades drawn in the room. I glanced at my phone and had 2 messages from my unexpected Super Bowl date. My Customer was already back in Europe. I decided to hit the gym sweat out the previous night's booze. Then it was up to the pool for an overpriced breakfast. I called Gene, his child hood friend and instructed him to meet me in the lobby at 2PM. Then I headed back to the room to shower and change. What to wear? Jerseys? None of my teams weren't playing. Shorts? It would be hot during the day but as the night wore on it probably drop to the mid 60's. We met in the lobby and he couldn't stop smiling. Are you really going to let me use his ticket? I told him yes, but he surely wasn't my first choice or even in the top 10. I might as well set the stage correctly if I was going to spend the next 10 hours with him. We hailed a cab to the Stadium and he gladly paid. We asked for his number since we knew it would be a zoo once the game was over.

As we walked closer to the Sun Life Stadium we could see that there were huge band stages set up and food trucks everywhere. It was one big tailgate. The atmosphere was electric. All the venues were open to the fans. There were no other tickets needed. There were already 20 to 30 thousand people there at 3 PM. There was a line of limos waiting to get through the check points. We waited on line at the first security checkpoint which was unusually quick. Once again, the rules no bags or coolers but cell phones were allowed. They weren't as strict as the first Game in Tampa where they wouldn't allow cameras. Then we walked into this tent that had to be an acre wide. We zig zagged through the lines to get to the front again it wasn't that crowded. There was a retired couple just in front of us. They were diehard lifetime Saint fans who had driven from Louisiana and purchased tickets when they arrived in Florida. They were so excited and dressed in their teams' colors of black and gold, head to toe. They asked us to take their picture when they reached the front of the line with the Stadium rising above them as the backdrop. They were giddy as school kids on their first trip to Disneyland. The ticket taker asked for their tickets, so they could scan them with their hand-held readers. They struggled to take them out of their lanyards they had around their necks. he scanned the first ticket and it made a low toned buzz noise then she tried again with the same result. They called over a Supervisor. Another ticket agent waived us over and scanned our tickets. She scanned both we heard a "Beep" and she tore off the bottom portion and said enjoy the game.

I looked back and could hear the supervisor saying there was nothing they could do since the tickets were counterfeit. I overheard the man attempting to argue his point. This can't be! His wife was in tears, and the man was standing there in utter disbelief. The official Super Bowl tickets have watermarks and holograms. The NFL goes the extra yard to protect against counterfeits. I'm not sure if these fans realized this. You must acquire tickets from a reliable source. I felt terrible for these fans but there wasn't much anyone could do at this point. Caveat Emptor …Buyer beware never rang truer than that day. The emotional swing that these poor people suffered was tantamount to leading a game for 58 minutes only to lose by a last-minute Field Goal.

Chapter 15 When The Saints Go Marching In!

It was about 4pm and I was starving. We walked past the encased Lombardi Trophy where everyone was posing for selfies. It was surrounded by security guards and placed on a 5ft platform surrounded by bullet proof glass. It was a shrine to the game. Fans clamored to get close. They had large wooden cutouts of players where you would stand behind and put your face where their heads were supposed to be and take pics.

Finally, the food venues we purchased pulled pork sandwiches and chicken BBQ. I'm not sure if Gene paid but I made it clear to keep my drink full once we got inside, after all he was getting a $2100 ticket for free. We went through some of the tents listened to several bands until 5:30. It was time to go inside. The outside activities seemed to be dominated by the New Orleans Saints fans. It almost felt as if it would be a Home game for them.

We went through one more checkpoint then glanced at our tickets for our seat assignments. We were in the end zone about 25 rows up. The place was starting to fill up and the players were on the field doing their pre-game warmups. Gene went to the bathroom and game back with two beers. I told him Vodka or Scotch from now on as I didn't want to be running back and forth to the bathroom and miss the game.

The stage was set for my 4th Super Bowl. Instead of my brothers or best friends I was sitting with a red headed stranger from Long Island. The Indianapolis Colts came into the game at 14-2 led by Quarterback Peyton Manning. The New Orleans Saints had a 13-3 winning record and were coached by Sean Peyton. It was the battle of the Peyton's the saints QB was Drew Brees an extremely accurate passer. They had running back Reggie Bush who had won the Heisman Trophy a few years earlier*.

In the press box Phil Simms, the former Superbowl winning QB for the NY Giants would call the game along with Jim Nantz. It was broadcasted on CBS in the US as well as 80 other countries. Over 100 million would watch the game in the States. Commercial set a record high at $2.8 million for a 30 second spot. Queen Latifah accompanied by an orchestra and chorus would sing America the Beautiful. Carrie Underwood the American Idol Winner, sang the National Anthem. It was an open Stadium so there was sure to be a flyover. If that was enough excitement The WHO would play the halftime show.

Once again, the culmination of the three day build up where things seem to go slow now changed. Everything was timed and well-orchestrated. Time starts to speed up. The singers sing, the planes fly over, and the coin gets tossed. It's basically a blur. Then the long-anticipated kickoff.

Suddenly, I hear this high-pitched sound almost siren like. About five rows behind us is this African American Saints fan wearing a Jersey and a large Whistle Shaped Hat. His fingers are in his mouth and the sound is deafening. I tell you if I had a crystal wine glass it would have shattered. There must have been 100 dogs lined up outside that stadium from surrounding towns. If this Human Whistle did it when the teams were down by our end zone the players would think the play was called dead. I never heard someone whistle that loud in 46 years. I had to plug my right ear every time the Saints scored otherwise I'd surely be deaf by halftime!

The Saints won the coin toss. The Whistle sounded. Then it was all Colts as the first quarter closed out it was Colts 10 and Saints zero. My ear drums were still intact. The second quarter the Saints Defense held the Colts to unchanged. The Saints offense managed to score two Field Goals. It was 10-6 at halftime. Now I had experienced some incredible Super Bowls. Perhaps I was spoiled. Sooner or later I would experience one that would be one sided it's the nature of the beast. So far this was a boring game. I ran to the bathroom and returned to my seat to see the Who perform for about a half an hour. I'm not a big WHO fan but I recognized most of the songs and enjoyed the concert. So, there I sat with my new buddy Gene waiting for the smoke to clear from the pyrotechnics. It was 10-6 and about a half a dozen high pitched screeching whistle. The Saints needed a spark. During the season they were a high powered, high scoring offense. Today they had been stymied by the Colts Defense led by their star defensive end Dwight Freeney.

The Saints had won the coin toss at the beginning of the game, but they opted to play defense first. Since the Saints scored right before halftime the Colts were set to receive the ball fist. The Saints decided to catch the Colts off guard by doing an onside kick to start the half. No one in the stadium expected that. If they didn't recover the ball after it went 10 yards they would give Peyton Manning and the Colts a short field to work with. It was a calculated risk in a regular season game. But to do it in the Super Bowl that took Big Balls. The Saints executed perfectly and gained possession. Drew Bree marched his team down the field 58 yards and performed a textbook check down pass to his back out of the backfield. Running Back Pierre Thomas caught the pass on the run and scored a 16-yard touchdown. Just like that the Saints were ahead 13-10. By now I knew to plug both ears as the Human Whistle exploded in cacophony. Football is a game of Momentum. *Old man Mo* just walked over to the Saints Sideline.

The Colts along with 80,000 attending fans in were in a state of shock. They had dominated the first half but were losing the game. Manning buckled up his chin strap and got to work. He drove his team 76 yards in 10 plays. Just like that 17-13 after they scored a touchdown.

They scored too fast as there was 6:05 left in the quarter. The Saints marched right down the field but were held to their 3rd field goal. The game was 1716 as the Colts held a narrow lead. Then a television timeout before the 4th quarter commences. Whoever takes the 4th quarter wins the game it's that simple. The weight lifting over the Winter, the Summer practices, the pre-season, the Grueling 16 game schedule, the playoffs and it comes down to 15 minutes. The finality of it all can be crushing. Your entire life focused on becoming a modern-day Gladiator. The dreaming of "GETTING TO THE SHOW" and becoming victorious as win your last game. Every kid that loves Football dreamt of it. We would act out the final seconds of the Super Bowl on the streets of NYC playing on the asphalt. I dreamed of it when we played number 1 in the country's Moeller HS in 1977. We dreamt of it in 1978 when our HS team went undefeated 9-0 and were NYC Champions. The odds of getting to the SHOW as a player and winning a Super Bowl are astronomical. It all comes down to 900 seconds just 15 minutes. Every play becomes more important every mistake is highlighted. It's so unforgiving, it's so unfair the finality of it all. Now the game begins to slow down. It's almost as if it's in slow motion. It's Pure Theater where not even the most seasoned Broadway Director could imagine or orchestrate the outcome. This is why you expend all this effort to be there in person.

The unheralded Saints Defense had held Peyton Manning's prolific Offense to just 17 points. Peyton leads his Colts down the field and the Saints stop them. The Colts kicker misses a 51-yard Field Goal and the score remains 17-16 as he Colts cling to a 1-point lead. Drew Brees takes the field and brilliantly mixes up run and pass plays. It successfully culminates with a 2-yard Touchdown to his Tight End Jeremy Shockey the ex- NY Giant. The Saints successfully go for the 2-point conversion and pull ahead 24-17.

Manning again takes the field but unfortunately throws a pick six and Tracy Porter returns it for 76 yards. This ices the cake. Interceptions can be crushing at this stage in the game. But a pic six return for a touchdown by an opponent is a dagger to the heart. The underdog New Orleans Saints win their first Super Bowl in come from behind fashion. What a game! Truly epic. Fireworks explode, Confetti Cannons erupt. The place is euphoric as fans march around under umbrellas as if they are in the French Quarter celebrating Mardi Gras on Bourbon St. The Band strikes up when the Saints Come Marching in. Drew Brees holds his 3-year old son with his newly adorned a Super Bowl champion cap. He stares into the camera and says I'm Going to Disneyland!

My seatmate Gene leans into me and says something. To this day I'm not sure what the hell he said as I was clinically deaf by the time the game ended. Whistle man's beloved team had won, and he was ecstatic. What a game! As for Gene, I never saw him again…

Pic Below Super Bowl Miami 2010

Chapter 16

"Whistle Monsta" gets his 15 minutes of Fame!

I wake early and read the Miami Herald. Once again, the front pages exclaim One of the Best come from behind Super Bowls in history as the New Orleans saints beat the World Champion Indianapolis Colts 34-17. The local TV station blurts out the same message. I was so fortunate to experience another great game.

In the paper, there was a picture of the Saints Super Fan "Whistle Monsta." The story went on to explain that his whistle can go over 120 decibels. That is the equivalent of a chainsaw or a thunderclap during a Summer storm. It is high enough to break a wine glass. He can whistle using any of his 10 fingers in a combination. He emulates a range of whistles from a Mocking Bird to a Referee Whistle. The Whistle Monsta Super Fan's name is Leroy Mitchell. His uncle taught him how to whistle as a kid. He is a fixture at Saints home games. He crafted a giant metal whistle that is attached to a Saints Helmet. He paints his face Black and Gold and dresses in NO Saint's uniform.

Over the next couple of weeks', he appeared on MTV and Good morning America. Jimmy Kimmel commented on him being one of the most unique mascots. After the Super Bowl the team signed his whistle. Andy Warhol would be proud as he received his 15 minutes of Fame.

On the plane ride home, I reflected as usual. It was my fourth Super Bowl. Everyone was unique. I would return home and spend hours telling the stories and explaining how certain events unfolded. There is always an air of spontaneity about each trip that makes it even more exciting. It's not just the Game. Although that is the focus. It's the people you meet and the experiences that unfold as game time approaches. You never know who you are going to meet or how the days prior to the Game will unfold. You must be open to what life brings you. Someone once said to me: Life is what happens when you plan. When you reflect on this simple statement you realize that even the best-laid plans can unravel. Don't lament, complain or throw in the towel. You must be able to adopt and adjust on the fly. In the end what was supposed to happen does.

I arrive in Newark at 7 pm and head to valet parking to retrieve my car. I find myself laughing from time to time a I reflect on the funny things that occurred. Tuesday morning it's back to the grind. Wouldn't it be awesome to capture the excitement to bottle it to sell it to those fans that don't have the opportunity or means to experience it in person? Imagine if that was feasible.

Whistle Monsta!

Chapter 17 Best Seats In The House!

It's March 2010, I'm on a plane to Geneva, Switzerland for Business. It's a long flight and luckily, I'm in first class. I scurry through security and stop at the Hudson News stand which is standard at any airport terminal in the US. I pick up the usual gum a newspaper and browse through the magazines and books. The magazines are all $3 to $5 dollars newspapers $1 to $3 dollars. There's a ton of romance Novels There are some NY Times Best Sellers in hard covers for $18 bucks and up on the front table. I wish I had time to read the reviews, but the plane is waiting. I impose my self-control as I have bought books before on impulse only to end up in the half-read pile on my desk at home. What if there was a fairly-priced book that would appeal to Football fans? Something that was engaging and informational with great anecdotes? Suddenly, I felt like that picture in the cartoon. Where the light bulb is sketched over the characters head in a bubble. What if other frequent travelers agreed with my conclusions? We all just want something good to read to pass the time away while on the tarmac or in the air. Something we could read to drown out the noise of fasten your seatbelt and escape the confines of this flying aluminum cage for the next few hours.

I have my laptop out and after reviewing some work emails and going over some charts. I begin to think what If I wrote a book sharing my experiences about going to 4 Super Bowls? I write about Markets and Equities every day, but I have never written a book. I started to compile some notes on my laptop before nodding off.

I check into the hotel and go meet my customer for lunch. We discuss business and spend the rest of the day trading back at his office on the shore of Lake Geneva. The next day we drive up to the top of this mountain we are at the foothills of the Alps. We relax in a field full of cows as these crazy Swiss and French Daredevils jump off the cliffs attached to colorful parasails and glide effortlessly into the valley below.

He is doing well are both on the same page as the World Equity Markets are headed higher. We never even discuss the past Super Bowl as it's water under the bridge at this point. Ironically, he was a NY Jets fan as he had grown up close to Shea Stadium in Queens. This is where the Jets originally played, prior to moving to moving into the Meadowlands in New Jersey. After living in Europe for a while he transitioned into more of a Soccer fan as it was difficult to watch American Football with the extreme time zone differences.

He was excited to go to a Soccer match in Germany that was coming up shortly. He mentioned that another Broker or what I refer to as "pigeons" had acquired some great seats down low in the stadium. I had met this Broker before and was actually a big fan as we had some extremely funny nights out together. I said I hope you have a great time and enjoy the game. We drove back to town walked through the old section of Geneva and picked up wine and meats to grill back at his apartment. The "Pre-war" section of Geneva is hilly with multi- Century old Buildings that rise from the cobblestone streets. They are adorned with wooden shutters. You get this eerily feeling that a German Panza Tank is going to come over the hill and roll down the street at any time. We stop at his favorite Italian restaurant & Pizza joint where he speaks to the proprietor in Italian. The owner glances at me and extends his hand with a slice of pizza and says Buena Sera. We pick up pasta and head back to his flat. On the walk home, I asked him what did you say to the owner back at the restaurant? He said I told him that you were an actor from the United States. That I was a hitman on the Sopranos for two seasons, but I had gotten whacked. I laughed and from then on whether we were in Rome, France or Switzerland that was the story we went with. I was even going to make up phony head shots the pictures that actors leave behind when they go on casting calls.

Monday afternoon we exchange goodbyes and I catch a cab to the airport. I try to sleep much of the way home and never even open my laptop on the 9hour flight home. Once again it was back to the grind.

It must have been about a month later, I receive a call at 4:15 in the morning. It's been my experience, that a phone call in the middle of the night are never good. Either way, I always leave my phone on in case my children need me in an Emergency situation. Waking up disorientated I scramble for my I Phone. I hear it's me Bob you're not going to believe what happened. I groggily reply Who? What happened? Who is this as I wipe my eyes? I realize it's my customer from Europe he is calling me from Germany. He said they rented an RV drove to Germany to see this exclusive Soccer Match. Everything was going fine. They park the RV they tailgate. The Pigeon had traded up for great seats. They were offered to the head Boss, but he refused an wanted to sit with his sons. So, my customer and the Pigeon gladly decided to use the Prime seats. They got on the long line to enter the stadium. Like ants heading back to the hill single file as they zigged and zagged through the maze. All you heard was beep, beep, with the occasional Vile Spa (Have FUN in German mixed in). The line was moving. Beep , beep, beep Vile Spa beep beep Zonk! Try again Zonk Zonk. Step to the side please. A German police officer with a huge German Shepard Dog heard the noise and moved closer to investigate. In Germany, they frown on scalping and counterfeit tickets a little bit more than in the US. Before they knew it, they were handcuffed and moved to the side of the line. How humiliating what if the Boss agreed to sit in those seats? My customer spoke Italian but not German. Once there was a bunch of fans who were in the same circumstance they were led to a holding cell deep beneath the cavernous soccer stadium.

So, they all stood side by side, handcuffed with zip ties in a cold damp cell. They were inside the bowels of the stadium they could hear the crowd cheering and the long melodious soccer chants, but they couldn't see a thing.

Several hours after the game ended the tunnel doors swung open and half of the alleged perpetrators were led out like cattle to old bus with caged windows. Just as my customer was about to be led away the Pigeon who was extremely claustrophobic begged him to get a valium he had hidden in his shoe. My customer looked at him in total distain and instructed him to F@#k off. It was 4:30 in the morning before I hung up the phone. I have to say that was one the best middle of the night calls I ever received it took me 20 minutes to stop laughing and fall back asleep.

It doesn't matter what event you're going to. There is always a scam. It doesn't matter what country. You must acquire your tickets either from the original source or a reputable ticket broker.

Chapter 18

Friends Come & Go But Teams are Forever

I believe the longer you live the more characters you meet. People come in and out of your life for reasons. Over the past 50 Years or so I had several best friends or close buddies. Growing up there was my neighbor Charlie he was like my 4th brother. He was always around to hang around with. He lived 5 houses away. We were in the Boy Scouts together played sports in the street and the school yard. We attended the same High School. We both ended up working on Wall St. and spent a lot of time at the Jersey Shore. Once he was married he moved to North Jersey and I rarely ever saw him again. One day he showed up at my front door carrying a work satchel and my kids nicknamed him Mailman Charlie. He remains a life-long friend to my brothers and myself.

Then there was Dino. He was an Italian kid from Chicago. Ironically, he was in the same class as my younger brother Chris when they got their seats on the Board of Trade. This is where they trade Bond Futures in Chicago. He moved to Rumson after a brief stint in London. I met him on the boat around 2000 and we became instant friends. He had this charisma about him combined with that Chicago swagger. He always dressed sharply and had a cigar in his hand whenever he had a chance. He had the perfect name DINO. If you had a name like Dino, you had to pull it off. He did it effortlessly. Everybody liked Dino. How could you not? His smile and demeanor were infectious. He and his wife Cathy have 3 daughters. Our kids attended Holy Cross Grammar School together. We rode the ferry together daily. We were always laughing and having a good time. We attended the Charity Cancer Balls and School events. I would cook from scratch for 20 people at his house just for fun.

One day, I asked Dino what sports he played in High school? He replied: that he was on the Rodeo team. Being from Brooklyn I could hardly contain myself and burst out laughing. What did you just say? He said I was on the Rodeo team. Stunned I was at a loss for words and just busted out laughing. If Tuck was there he would have shredded him. Trying to stop laughing I inquired what was your specialty. Without skipping a beat, he said “Calf Roping.”

Now he was getting a little bit perturbed as the blood rushed to his face and his cheeks reddened. He beckoned for his wife. Cathy! Cathy! Where’s my roping can? She said I don’t know I think it’s on a shelf in the basement. Hun, can you get it for me? She leaves the kitchen to retrieve what looked like a women’s hat box. She produces a round shaped box covered in dust. He then instructs me to come outside with him. He opens the can and withdraws a lasso. He starts plying the encased Lasso to make it more pliable. He unravels the rope puts his cigar in his mouth and instructs me to start walking away from him at a brisk pace. Suddenly I feel a sting on my right ankle as if I had just got whipped. He barks out, I missed do it again. Now I'm not as enthused as I was on the first attempt. I walk away from him I feel something hit my ankle then its drawn taught. On the second attempt he roped my right ankle. He hadn't done this in at least 25 years and there I was Roped in. That was Dino! A Cool customer, a straight shooter, a Wall St buddy and a Great Husband and Dad.

I realized he really was a cowboy from Indiana. Shortly after that we bought a quarter horse together named Star. The kids loved him. Unfortunately, Dino died of a Heart attack at the age of 50. He was a great friend that we all miss every day.

So, I'm in NJ only 14 years and I lose two great friends. Not exactly a good track record. First Tucker then Dino both great guys. I will always remember and appreciate the time spent with them. There's a lesson to be learned. Carpe Diem! Latin for seize the day. Enjoy every moment no regrets.

The summer of 2011 rolls around I'm living in Monmouth Beach. We belong to Little Monmouth Beach Club and we live in the middle of town. Kerry new friend of mine says you have to meet this new guy who moved into town His name is Mario. You two are cut from the same cloth. In May, she invites me to Avenue a beachfront restaurant. There is Mario with his posse of about 6 guys. He hands me an Expresso Martini and we all raise our glasses and toast to the beginning of the Summer. He had just moved into an older Beach Mansion called *White Columns*. The local surfers called it windows as it had these enormous 12-foot windows that overlooked the Atlantic Ocean. He invited me over for a barbeque. I attended with my two children. We walked over the seawall and we played Bocce on the beach. We could only play at low tide as the ocean would hit the seawall at high tide.

Back at the house I met his other friends and we all helped cooking and entertaining. It wasn't long after this that we renamed "White Columns" to the "Resort". Needless to say, it was a great Summer. When the days grew shorter and the temperatures cooled, Football Season had arrived. Ironically, Mario who had grown up in Newark, NJ was a NY Jets fan. Just like me he had the "Jets Curse"! Now it had been 42 years since the Jets had won a Super Bowl led by the brash young Quarterback Joe Namath. Mario had season tickets right on the 50 Yard line. We shared stories of going to games over the past decades. He knew I was a real fan who had endured epic let downs over the past 4 decades. As Jet fans we were all in this together. White Collar, Blue Collar, Old and Young we all had the "Curse". Sooner or Later our beloved team would win. We were loyal fans. It's as if we lived by the Postman's Credo. Rain, Snow and Blazing Sun we showed up only to endure

4th Quarter leads slowly disappear. Same Old Jets. Yet we came back the next Sunday. They were our team and we supported them. *J-E-T-S! Jets , Jets, Jets!* 80,000 fans chanted in unison!

What is it that keeps a fan loyal all these years. Is it an American thing? The Boston Red Sox have a cult like following. It was over 85 years before the Curse of the Bambino was broken. Babe Ruth was traded to the Yankees in the 1919. The Owner Harry Freeze needed money to shore up his failing Broadway Show.

The Chicago Cubs curse lasted 71 years. Billy Goat Tavern owner William Sianis cursed the team after he was thrown out of Wrigley Field for bringing his pet goat mascot named Murphy to the game.

In Hockey, the NY Rangers were a great team winning two Stanley Cups in 1933 and 1940. After the 1940 win the owners paid off the Mortgage to Madison Square Garden and burned it in the Stanley Cup trophy. Some hockey fans feel they had desecrated the "CUP" and the Hockey Gods punished the NY Rangers. Chants of "1940"could be heard in Madison Square Garden for 55 Years!

I'm sure that Sports Psychologists have studied these phenomena for years. I believe it's an analogy for life in America. You come here you work every day. You hold on to core beliefs your loyal and you root for the Underdog. Because inevitably, one day you will succeed. Life is comprised of Winners and Losers. Emotions of Hope and Fear. Who wants to live their life in Fear? That seems like a terrible way to start off every morning. This is America where you have the opportunity to succeed. We want to see people achieve their goals. We want our teams to win. I think deep down everyone Hopes to become a Winner. So, every season we come back. Whether it's a form of escapism or entertainment, we arrive early, we gather with friends we tailgate and celebrate our teams. We throw the ball around we dream of one day being a champion.

Someday before I've gone to the other-side. Yes, before I die, I will get to see them win a Superbowl! It would be the most cherished Deja Vue ever. I close my eyes I relive my childhood on that Fall day. It was 1970, I was wearing my Jets tee shirt. We were playing Football on the hot Staten Island Asphalt. I was QB, I dropped back as the last seconds ticked off the clock. I shed one tackle. I threw it deep. My Brother caught it and ran into the endzone. The underdog Jets beat favored Baltimore Colts. J-*E-T-S …JETS, JETS, JETS! If only…*

Pic above My children Ally & Steve at their 1st Jet Game together

Fall Tailgate at Met Life with Mario and crew

Chapter 19 Stay By The Phone!

It's the Summer of 2012 and we spent most of the time at the beach. Monmouth Beach is a small Beachfront community with the ocean on one-side and the bay on the other. It's not quite a barrier Island but close. The town consists of a Church, a bank, a gas station a couple of restaurants and shops In 2011, we had a serious Hurricane hit the New Jersey Shore called Irene. Most of the town flooded. Some houses suffered flood or wind damage. I lived on one of the high points in town and the house I was in suffered no damage. Boats were cast aside like toys in the local marinas.

I helped my buddy bail out his basement and get his house back in order. We decided to put a Volleyball court on the beach and get some exercise during the day. We were basically a crew of old dudes that would challenge anyone to a game. It was originally a plan to keep us from drinking beer but it's kind of took on a life of its own. Either way it was a great Summer. As the days grew shorter, Summer turned into Fall and the beach crowd diminishes. It's now "Local Summer". We have the place to ourselves once again. September is one of the best months at the Jersey Shore as the water remains warm. Who knew this would be the calm before the storm. It was late in October when the barometric pressure dropped and Hurricane Sandy which had formed off the coast of

Africa was gaining strength. After dealing with Hurricane Irene a year earlier I couldn't believe we were in the crosshairs for the second consecutive year. It was then I learned that Hurricanes are mutually exclusive. It didn't matter what happened previous year. Sandy made landfall on October 29, 2012 as a direct hit to the Jersey Shore causing over 30 Billion Dollars in damage.

Prior to the storm arriving around 3PM . I battened down the hatches at the Resort. I started both generators as the power went out and left town driving my 4/4 Pickup straight down a flooded Ocean Ave. The waves sounded like a Freight Train as they barreled over the 12-foot seawall. I had trouble controlling my truck as the water was up to the floor boards. Debris was flying everywhere. I made it up to the Parkway, but the Governor had declared a State of Emergency and closed it.

I switched over to Rt 18 and drove to Rt 70 to check on my parents in Tom's River. The roads were empty. Just then I heard a loud explosion. I was blinded by a piercing blue arcing light. Was this it. Was I dead?

I remember jamming on the brakes. When my eyes refocused. I again saw the blue light and now it was accompanied by red and orange flames. I learned later that a Transformer had exploded. I drove the last 5 miles and made it to their home to check on them.

The next day I returned to carnage there were houses off their foundations and boats in yards. There were 10- foot sand dunes on Ocean Ave. Electricity would be out for weeks. Halloween was cancelled. We had National Guardsman posted on all the bridges entering town to protect us from looters.

I stayed for a week and helped Mario and other neighbors get their homes functioning. Then I headed north with my children for a couple of days as the weather was turning colder. When I returned I back fed my electric panel with a generator. So at least I had minimal electric and I could turn on the heat. I was lucky as I sustained little damage just more of an inconvenience. Others had lost everything.

Mario and I worked long days to get his house back in shape and to acquire gas for the generators. There was a shortage of gas and we had to use our ingenuity to avoid waiting on long lines. I donated clothing and other necessities to families in Sea Bright who had lost everything. It was a tough time. The rallying cry became Jersey Strong! The state recovered it just took some areas years to regain a sense of normalcy.

Before you knew it Christmas and New Year's flew by. It was late January when I received a call from Mario. It was quick all he said was stay by your phone and answer when I call. I must premise this by stating that I'm not one of those people that is tied to his phone. So, him giving me a warning was his way of averting this. Usually when he does this it's a good sign we are about to go on some crazy adventure.

It's Wednesday night, the phone rings I pick up and he says I may have an extra ticket to the Super Bowl this weekend do you want to come. Who says no to that?

He says let me finish. I may have a spot on a private jet for the ride back, but you must get down there on your own. I say great where is it? It's in New Orleans. Piece of cake!

Hurricane Sandy destroyed my old cabana

Chapter 20 Is there any room at the Inn?

After Mario's invitation, I hit the phones. It's late so I'll figure out where to stay when I get down there since its only for 1 night. I only need airfare as I have the most important piece of the equation , the elusive Super Bowl ticket. The Super Bowl is February 3, 2013 in New Orleans. I know the lay of the land since this is my 4th time in New Orleans. This is going to be easy. Friday night I get a call from Mario. He explains his travel plans and that he will be in NOLA on Sunday around 1 pm. I pack light, cell phone, computer, two changes of clothes all in a carry on bag. I fly Continental to Houston then Southwest to NOLA. At this point, I could do this in my sleep. I arrive in New Orleans around 2 PM Saturday 28 hours before kickoff. Now it's time to showcase my procurement skills.

I exit the plane and make a bee-line for the taxi stand. Uber wasn't the rage yet. The long line moves slowly. I survey the passengers glancing at their cell phones. I ask the people behind me if anyone would prefer to split a cab to the casino downtown. A tall thin man 4 people behind me states he is going that way and jumps to the front of the line to get in the awaiting cab with me. On the way there we make small talk. I inquire are you here for the game. He affirms and states that he is here from the Tech Company Akamai. He explains they are attempting to stream the Super Bowl for the first time. I inform him that I am a Technical

Analyst and that I love AKAM which is trading around $40 a share. I ask him for his business card and tell him I'll send him a chart when I return to the office. Being a tech-geek, he agrees and relinquishes his card.

The taxi pulls up adjacent to a high-rise hotel across the street from the new casino. We get out and he offers to pay for the cab ride as he is expensing it. I ask where he is staying, and he points to the hotel in front of us. I watch as he disappears into the lobby. Just then I see Ex-Football Coach and Broadcaster John Gruden. I yell his name and he waves as he also enters the Lobby. Bingo! Eureka! The lightbulb goes off. I enter the hotel and the place is crawling with Baltimore Ravens fan. There is a café packed with people wearing their purple and black jerseys. In the middle of the lobby there is this huge towering 10story atrium where you can see people walking around the floors above. Smack in the middle there is a 3-story escalator that leads to the 3rd floor lobby. I work myself through the crowd, board the open-air escalator. I put my game face on as I disembark and get on the line. After I hear next please, I approach the desk. I ask the young lady for a room and she laughs saying this is Baltimore Ravens Headquarters and it's been booked for over a year by the league. I keep a straight face, I am totally dismissive but not rude. I said this is an emergent situation and I need to speak to the manager.

The manager meanders over with this inquisitive look on his face. It's now or never. It's time to pull my bluff. Managers are usually accommodating but can be cocky especially in situations such as these. I flash my newly acquired business card and explain I just flew in from NY to ensure that the games streaming goes off without a hitch. I know they always keep a couple of rooms for emergencies and this falls into that category. I'm making a bet that he knows Akamai workers are staying here. He knows its all-league and TV people staying there. Remember, I already gathered the information on my recon on the ride over in the cab. Its Baltimore Raven Head Quarters, John Gruden the game analyst is there, Akamai employees are there. The pieces of the puzzle fit. My story isn't that farfetched. He looks at my card and states let me see what I can do. Now he is the manager I'm betting he won't book my room he will let the clerk do it. If he books the room, he will see that my credit card doesn't match my business card and the bluff is called and I'm back pounding the pavement.

The next part takes balls. He returns and says he has one room for Saturday night and it's $650 dollars. I thank him profusely for his effort. Then I inform him I must step away and call my supervisor to make sure that I'll be reimbursed. He acknowledges this and instructs the girl to hold the room for me. When he walks away I return and inform the front desk clerk that I'll take it. Just like that the bluff worked I have a room in downtown New Orleans across from the Casino. No Irish Bayou this time!

Chapter 21 Blackout Shades, Blackout Bowl

I enter the room take a shower then a nap. I call my old trader who now lives in NOLA. He informs me they are at some bar eating crawfish, the place is packed with players and fans. By the time I arrive its 6:30 the place is cleared out just a bunch of drunks. We catch up have some Dixie Beers and crawfish. They extend a dinner invitation to me. I ask where and how many people he says 11 people and names a few restaurants. I laugh as I stop him in his tracks. There is no freekin way, that you could get a table for 11 people in any restaurant within a 15-mile radius.

As we leave the warehouse district I see Emeril's. I tell him I'm going home showering changing and I'm going here for dinner. Now it's his turn to laugh saying I have trouble getting in there and I live here! I head back to the hotel determined to prove him wrong. I shower change and retrace my tracks. At this point it's about 8:15. I work my way through the front door and crowded hostess stand. I get to the bar it's 4 deep. I ask for someone to hand me the wine list as I inch closer. It's been over 20 years since I've first been to NOLA. Tonight, is going to be my night that I finally eat at Emeril's. Now I'm two people away. I ask the young lady in front of me to relay my request. I order a bottle of Chardonnay and a nice California Cabernet to start. I pass through my credit card with a $50-dollar tip. I inform the bartender that I'd like to eat at the bar. I talk to those around me and I meet a tall brunette female Dentist from Tulane and share my plan to eat at the bar. After about an hour with their help I pull up a barstool. I made it I'm finally going to eat at the famed Emeril's. I share the white wine with those around me. They are enamored with my NY accent. They are inquisitive and before you know I'm giving out investment advice. The place is crawling with celebrities and sports starts. Next to us the former Linebacker Jack del Rio who had just been released as a Head Coach. I lean over and introduce myself and tell him he was one of my favorite players and I'm sure that he would get another opportunity to be a Head Coach. He thanked me for the kind words and was enjoying talking and engaging with the crowd. John Travolta walk in with a buddy and was ushered to the back as other patrons waited patiently.

Then Jim the financial analyst from TV appears behind me and people are asking him for advice. I lean in and said just tell them to buy everything we are headed to 2000 on the S&P from its current level of 1200. He looks at me and I state I worked at Goldman also and was on CNBC for 9 years. That was about the extent of our conversation as he turned back towards the crowd.

Back at the bar the dentist and her friend could see I was excited to order. They started rifling off choices. I had to get the turtle soup, so that was ordered. Then Escargot followed by grilled Gulf snapper Cajun style and Duberge Cake for dessert. I was happy another box checked off in the journey of life.

After dinner another guy I met invited me to a bar outside of town where his crew was partying. They were on a float in a parade on Bourbon St. that took place earlier. He asked if I could convince the Dentist to come as he was dying to ask her out. Just like that I paid the bill and we were off to this bar. After I met all these characters in costumes and drank at their local watering home I realized it was 2 am. I had no idea where I was, but It was time to get back to the hotel. I hailed a cab and off I went. I often wondered did the dentist and the local ever end up together. Despite exchanging numbers, I never heard from them again.

Back at the room I drew the Blackout shades closed and hit the sack. I woke up to Mario's call at noon. Where are you? I told him the Hotel's name and That I'm across from the casino. He explains that the jet must go to Baton Rouge as there was no room to park the plane and no jet fuel left. He instructs me to meet him in the lobby at 1PM. I get up shower and head downstairs. New Orleans is always warm and humid as it sits right where the Mississippi meets the Gulf of Mexico. I grab a gatorade and a water to hydrate as I head outside into the sunny day. We are going to have to walk to the newly named Mercedes Stadium (The former Super Dome. No cars are allowed within a 1.5-mile radius. I meet Mario and his daughter along with his stock broker friend Roger. He informs me we must make one stop to pick up the tickets. Then we will head to the French Quarter to tailgate at the bars. I check my bag at the bell check to retrieve after the game. We secure the tickets at a nearby hotel from one of his good friends.

It's 4 hours till kick off we make it to the French Quarter. My old customer from Europe is down there and we attempt to connect. He confuses directions and has no patience. I inform him of my whereabouts, but he becomes exasperated and a bit belligerent. He already screwed up one Superbowl as I discussed earlier I wasn't going to let him do it again.

We stop at the 200-Year Old Absinthe Bar and indulge in a Vincent Van Gogh cocktail. We are walking down Bourbon St as his daughter asked why those girls are shouting from the balconies. What's the deal with the colored beads everyone is throwing. I turn her head away to distract her, as a girl lifts her shirt in an attempt have beads thrown her way. We continue down the street until we reach Brennan's Oyster House where we meet up with some pilot friends of Mario's. After putting a dent in a bushel of oysters and a half a case of beer we start walking again in the direction of the stadium. Everything was going off without a hitch. My 5th Super Bowl and my 3rd in NOLA. Everything was on auto pilot. Everything went smooth.

We arrive at the towering saucer like stadium that most had seen on TV when Hurricane Katrina made landfall a few years earlier. It had been refurbished since then. Once again Phil Simms and Jim Nantz will broadcast the game for CBS. A 30 second spot had jumped to $4 Million dollars.

We enter our seats are on the 40- yard line and we are sitting in the 30th row or so. The players are already on the field warming up. It would be Joe Flacco at the helm for the Baltimore Ravens offense and Ray Lewis for their defense. Colin Kaepernick was the elusive young QB for San Francisco. This was the first Super Bowl where I didn't have to pay for a ticket. I was Mario's guest. Alicia Keyes was scheduled to sing the National Anthem and Beyoncé was the halftime entertainment. We are in our seats the crowd is cheering and then the speed pics up again. All 71,000 rise and take our hats off. The National Anthem, the fireworks, the coin toss & the kickoff whistle all timed and according to schedule.

I have zero skin in the game and could care less who wins. My goal is to see a great game. It's Roger first Super Bowl he is wearing these oversized Christmas Ball ornaments. He is betting on everything from the coin toss outcome to the length of the National Anthem rendition. The game begins and it's as if the Baltimore Ravens were playing at home! Most of the fans in attendance go crazy every time they score which is quite often. It's 21-6 at Halftime and the Ravens are clearly dominating the contest. To be honest it's more fun watching the crowd. Sitting directly in front of us are die hard San Francisco fans with this stupid monkey they are passing around. They call it the Rally Monkey. I'm busting their balls because it's clearly not working as their team is down by three scores.

With a minute left I work my way out of the aisle and up to the restroom. I walk right by my customer who is 6 rows behind us. I'm so glad our seats are better! There are 71,000 people at the game. He couldn't find me in the French Quarter but just like that he is 6 rows behind me. Too funny, how ironic?

I pit stop at the restroom before the line grows out of control. I the try to get food at the concession but they are all abandoned. Beyoncé is about to perform. All you here is Queen Bae. I'm standing there in disbelief. All the workers left their posts behind the counters and have their cellphones above their heads recording her performance. What the hell? It's the biggest game of the year and I can't get any food at halftime? I see one vendor holding a hand-held cart that he goes down the aisles with. I yell I'll take two of whatever you are selling. He says $18 dollars and hands me to fried alligator sandwiches. It's at this point my stomach yearned for the Muffulettas sandwiches I brought to the last two Super Bowls in New Orleans. I work my way through the crowd which now includes all the workers in the stadium and manage to grab a beer off another walking vendor. Back in my seat. I share my slim pickens and await the second half.

I'm not a Beyoncé fan so I'm not sure what all the fuss is about. She finishes up the set the crowd goes wild. The smoke clears, and the second half kickoff ensues. The Ravens score another Touchdown and go up 28-6 early in the 3rd Quarter. Remember how I said everything was going so smoothly earlier? That was about to change.

Suddenly the lights in the Stadium go out. We were in total darkness on outside while auxiliary or lower than normal lighting was still visible across the field. The first feeling is surprise followed by disbelief. There is no announcement from the PA system. No one knows what's going on for certain. After about 5 minutes we discuss if this could be terrorism. I instruct Mario to hold onto his daughter stay on my six if we must get out of here quickly. I'm 6'1 265 while Mario is about 5'11 165. I've been in some panic situations before. He agrees then we call different people back home to get information. We must decide as to what action to take. Do we leave, or do we go by the exit and wait for further information? If it was indeed terrorism every second counts on how you react.

After several calls it was relayed to us that some transformer blew, and they were trying to patch into another energy source. We never panicked we devised a plan went with it. In emergency situations this is the proper cause of action to follow. Thank God it turned out to be just a transformer.

The Game was suspended for 34 minutes. Once play resumed it was if the two teams changed uniforms. The San Francisco 49ers scored 17 unanswered points to bring the score to 28-23. Could the "Rally Monkey" have caused the Blackout? Now it was the life of the party being passed around the rows. It was patted hugged and kissed. Up and down the row we all began to root for San Fran. In the 4th quarter the Ravens scored 2 field goals to make it 34 points while the 49ers scored another touchdown and trailed by 5. Colin Kaepernick marched the 49ers down the field to the Ravens 7-yard line but turned the Ball over on downs. They needed a touchdown to win as the score was 34-29. After the Ravens took over on downs San Frans Defense backed up the Ravens to their own Goal Line. With time running out the Ravens took a safety making the score 34-31. It was the first the Superbowl ended up on a self-inflicted safety to win the game.

The place went nuts! What was looking to be a lopsided victory turned out to be another incredible game where Momentum switched side after a 34 minute Blackout! We filed out into the streets it was very late as the blackout threw off all the scheduling. We walked back toward the riverfront with the rowdy crowd. Police in Riot gear and mounted cops on huge horses kept the peace. We made it back to our agreed upon rendezvous point. I went another two blocks back to Raven Head Quarters to retrieve my carry on. It was sheer pandemonium there. Traffic was a nightmare as the city was gridlocked with all these streets being closed prior to the game. It wasn't until 1:00 am that our limo arrived, and we headed to the Baton Rouge airport. It must have been close to 2:30 am when we reached the private jet. After the safety checks it was Wheels Up. What a Game!!!

Bourbon Street in front of the Absinthe Bar established 1808!

Mario, Danielle, Roger and Myself

Chapter 22 Faster than a Speeding Bullet

On the way home, the jet was cold I was sitting across from my buddy, he was spent. It was smaller jet with a 3-person crew and sat about 8 passengers. I was extremely grateful to get a ride home in such opulent fashion. Mario's daughter and Roger were across the aisle everyone was out cold. I asked the flight attendant for a little heat as all the blankets were already spoken for. I couldn't sleep I was still amped up from the last 48 hours. No one would ever believe the last two days and what had transpired. I reached for my bag and pulled out my laptop. It had been several years since I jotted down those notes about my first couple of times at the Super Bowl. I should add more I thought. I opened the laptop but couldn't find the files. Perhaps it was on the other one I had left at home. Either way I always had a great memory. I'm sure I could transcribe the events when I found the time.

I began to reflect on all the fun and adventures that transpired over the years at these 5 games. It really is amazing how these games turn out. Most of the times the two best teams get into the final game. Statistically they are very close in every fashion. It really comes does to how the individuals perform during that 1 hour. A minor mistake here or there can alter the outcome.

It appears we flew the whole way back at low altitude. I watched the sun come up as we approached the New Jersey border. Flying home straight after the game ended alleviated the hassle of getting a hotel room for another night. The convenience of flying private is unmatched. Forget about electric cars and autonomous vehicles. I look to the day when cars can fly.

We arrived at Morristown Airport. I thanked the crew for waiting for us and getting us back safely. I thanked Mario for an awesome game and said goodbye. On the way home, I was against traffic and headed straight to the office. I picked up my son from Holy Cross and told him all about the game. He was excited but also a bit jealous as he wants me to take him to a Super Bowl. I gave him the standard answer. When the Jets get in we are going! By now he started believing in the curse and stated that will never happen. I totally agreed with him but failed to acknowledge it.

Just like that another season ended. Now it was back the coldest month and figuring how to get somewhere warm before the Summer. The pic below shows the staggering amount of Private Jets stacked to capacity at New Orleans airport. The crew had to fly to Baton Rouge to refuel as NOLA ran out of jet fuel!

Chapter 23 The “Velvet Ropes” Game

Certain character traits are passed down through genes or inherited while others are learned. Over the years, my son listened & absorbed all my stories of attending live sporting events. I guess it’s my fault in a way that he wants to attend a Super Bowl. I can’t say I was surprised when he asked to go see Lebron James play for his 8th Grade Graduation present. I asked when? He said next week. I said it’s the NBA Finals in Miami. That’s a tall order! Let me see if I can work that out. I went on Stub Hub ticket exchange to check out the availability. Lebron James had left Cleveland three years ago to join an already stacked team with Chris Bosch and Dwyane Wade. They had won the championship under Coach Erik Spoelstra in 2012.

I asked my daughter if she wanted to go to Florida for a short vacation as she just finished her Freshman year in High School. She quickly jumped at the chance. I promised her a shopping spree while my son and I would attend the game. The Miami Heat were the defending Champs, and this would be game 6 against the favored San Antonio Spurs who were leading the series 3-2. Tickets weren’t that expensive as the Heat were trailing and not too many fans expected they could repeat the previous year’s success. I bought two tickets in the 38th row behind the basket.

We arrived at the Arena early and were issued white commemorative tee shirts to wear during the game. It was going to be a "White out" where the majority of those attending would be wearing white shirts to psyche out the opposing team. I had been to White out games at Penn State and they were incredible.

Shaquille O'Neal was interviewed before the game and was about 20 rows ahead of us. Our row was comprised of diehard Heat fans that were season ticket holders. They were surprised to see us sit in the seats rather than the original ticket holders. Once they saw us adorn the White Heat tee-shirts they warmed up to us. My son was grinning from ear to ear the crowd was rocking. The Heat had a great Defensive player and rebounder. He was a tall Caucasian heavily tattooed and sported a multi colored Mohawk. He was beloved by fans and nicknamed the *"BirdMan."* He talked the talk and walked the walk. He backed up his unique look with his outstanding play. In the upper deck, there were several people walking around with Giant Bird Wings and were highlighted on the Jumbotron whenever he made an outstanding play.

The crowd reached a fever pitch as the teams jumped for the opening tip. The San Antonio Spurs seemed to lead the entire game. The fans in our row never gave up or stopped cheering, A Latin guy 4 seats over kept moving his hands in a rhythmic twisting motion, his lips moved as he whispered indistinguishable words then would extend and yell something in Spanish. It appeared he was trying to put a spell on the San Antonio Spurs. It was the closest thing to Santeria I have ever experienced. If the game got slow, we could always watch our row mate practice his magic. The pace quickened and Lebron James put on a show for the ages as he scored a Triple Double!

It wasn't until the 4th Quarter when the Heat cut a double-digit lead to 3-points. The workers in the stadium had brought the Velvet Ropes into the tunnel and were easing towards court side. The Championship Trophy was ready to be presented to the San Antonio Spurs. The Velvet Ropes were utilized to cordon off the crowd. Many fans had already left the American Airlines Arena to beat the traffic home. There was 10 seconds left and security began to extend the Velvet Ropes and guard the sidelines from overzealous fans. Then one of the best clutch shots in NBA Finals occurred right in front of us. Ray Allen received a pass at the baseline and rose up to swish a 3-point shot. There was 5.2 seconds left and it was nothing but net. The Game was tied 95-95. The security and Velvet Ropes disappeared back into the tunnel.

Fans who had left tried feverishly to re-enter the stadium were turned away when all the doors were locked. The Arena was deafening. We high fived the whole row. We were family now! The game wasn't over yet. It was Overtime which was just as exciting. The Velvet Ropes began to creep out of the tunnel once again. Security manned the sidelines. With 1:43 to go Miami takes the lead 101 to 100 the heat ended up finally pulling ahead and won 103-100. I can't hear a thing as the fans erupt after witnessing one of the best NBA Final games in history. The Velvet Ropes disappear until game 7.

We exit the stadium and the disgruntled fans who left early and were denied re-entry, now joined in the jubilee. We navigate the crowded sidewalks to the parking lot. Local Television News trucks are there with their 20-foot satellite antennas fully extended. Reporters are looking for fan's reactions and first-hand accounts of what it was like inside the Arena. We jump in the car and get in line for the freeway entrance for our ride back to Ft Lauderdale where we are staying.

My son asks me if I think the Heat will win game 7. I say yes. It's just like the ball through Buckner's legs. His puzzling glance indicates he doesn't comprehend my analogy. I explain the1986 Boston Red Sox vs NY Mets World Series game 6 analogy that we discussed earlier.

The Red Sox were favored and winning the game before Bill Buckner the Red Sox First Baseman committed an error. It was similar to the Heat being the underdog in this series. Mookie Wilson hit a routine ground ball up the first base line and over the bag. It appeared Buckner looked at the runner on third for a split second. Perhaps his focus was compromised for a split-second. This allowed a ball to go through Bill Buckner's legs and into the outfield and letting the winning run cross the plate. The Mets won in the 10th inning forcing Game 7. In this case, Ray Allen was Mookie

Wilson. Ray Allen's clutch 3 Pointer tied the Game forcing Overtime. It demoralized their opponent. No one expected this to occur. Thousands of fans had left the arena and were banging on the doors to re-enter. This game 6 has been referred to the best Final Basketball game of all time!

In my opinion the 7th game of the World series in 1986, didn't have to be played as the Red Sox were so discouraged. I felt the Mets would surely win. As I stated previously, I attended that Game 7 in 1986 and watched the Mets win the World Series in epic come from behind fashion. He turns to me and says that's why you always say if you get a chance to go to Game 7 in any sport you should go. I reply with an emphatic YES! He says so we are going? I laugh as I realize the student had become the teacher. I said we won't be able to go since we are flying home Friday. He looks back at me and informs me the game is Thursday. Game 7 here we come!

We get home at 2 am. I pull out the laptop and buy 4 nose bleed upper deck seats for $400 a piece. Two days later we eat dinner and drive south to Miami. My two kids and a buddy.

The next day we see that the Velvet Ropes game made National news. They showed fans clamoring to re-enter a locked stadium and the pandemonium that ensued inside after Ray Allen's 3- pointer.

We arrive at the Arena about an hour early. Everyone is excited as we climb to our seats. The place is a mad house. The Spurs don't stand a chance. In the 4th quarter, the place erupts in mayhem. Miami staves off a late in the paint shot by Spurs center Duncan and Lebron James scores last basket to ice the game at 95-88. The Spurs were broken. The Spurs were the 1986 Red Sox. The game didn't have to be played. The kids were jumping up and down and celebrating. We exit the arena there must be a crowd of 20,000 people outside. My daughter wants to emulate the fans who are crowd surfing. She quickly changes her mind when a vicious fight breaks out right next to us. Both kids grab my arms as I barrel through the tumultuous crowd. We arrive at the car and get in. it takes us an hour to get on the freeway which is a 5-minute walk away. Overzealous fans are driving all over the place while their friends on the roofs or hoods of their cars waving Miami Heat Flags. We finally get home and decide to shoot off fireworks on the beach to celebrate their first Game 7. We get to bed its almost 3:30 am. Nothing like a Game 7!!!

It was Pure Magic!!!

This is a picture of the White out Shirt they gave us at Game 6

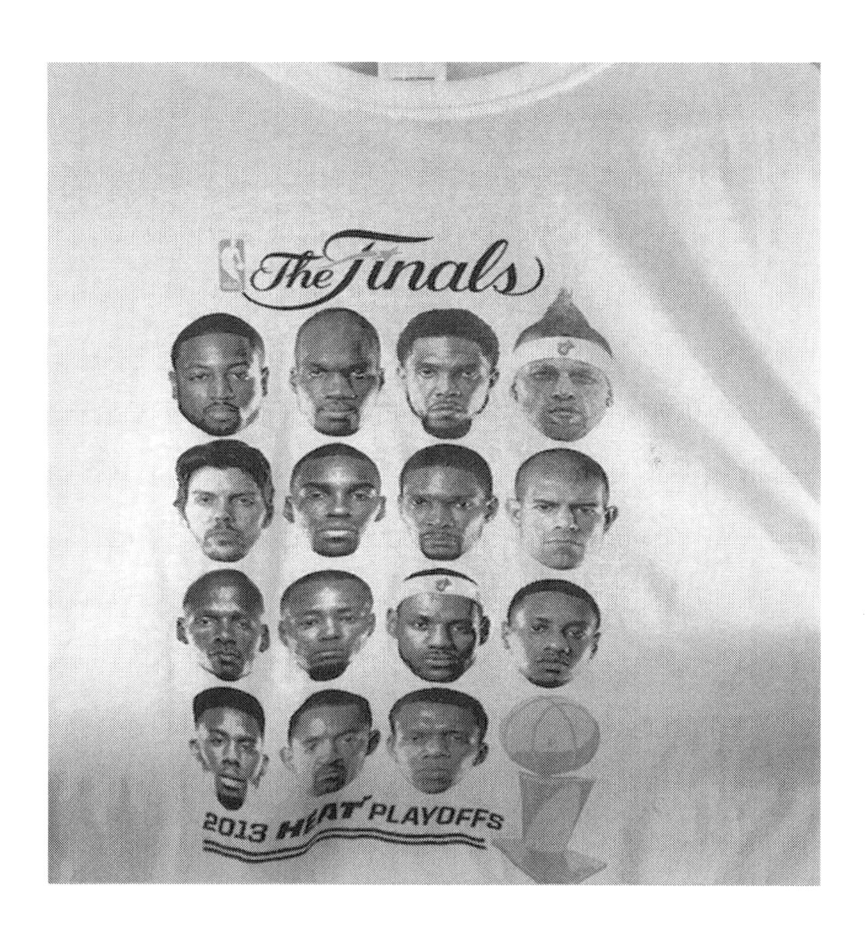

Chapter 24 Hometown Game

In October 2013, I go to a bar called "Big Shots" to meet Mario's crew to watch the Sunday games. A guy there is hawking Jerseys. I buy a Russell Wilson QB Seattle Seahawk Jersey for my son for 40 bucks. Mario laughs and bust my balls saying it's not real but a knock off. I jokingly inform him I'm done with the Jets. I'm switching teams and now I'm a Seahawk fan. I watched Russell play and the kid is masterful. He chides me some more. The next day my son comes home from school and the jersey is on his bed and he is ecstatic. He puts it on we go outside and throw the ball around. Little did I know that the Seahawks would go on a streak that would lead them to the show that year!

They announce that in 2014 Super Bowl XLVIII will be played outside in February in NJ Meadowlands at the NY Giants and NY Jets Home field. This would be the first Outside Super Bowl in a cold weather city. It's in our home Stadium. All the Jets must do is to win enough games to get in. We all talk about going but who the hell wants to pay two grand to watch a Football game outside in February. It's bad enough in December with temperatures falling!

The season plays out and two teams with the best records turn out to be the Denver Broncos and the Seattle Seahawks Both at 13-3. I bought my son a Seahawk Jersey and their Quarterback shreds Defenses' s across the league. Pete Carol the ex-NY Jets coach is now the Seattle Seahawks

Head Coach. Both the Jets and Seahawks have white and green in their uniforms. Both mascots fly. One is a jet the other is a bird. They are playing in the Meadowlands Stadium the NY Jets home field and Joe Namath is doing the coin toss. I'm now 51 years old is this as close as I'm going to get to a Jet's Super Bowl? I realize this is probably the best shot I have. My son's Birthday is February 19th. I pick him up from school and ask him how would he like to go to the Super Bowl for his Birthday? I looked in the rear-view mirror he was in shock. Are u kidding me? His smile was infectious as I said we are going just you and me buddy. We must dress warm it's February in the Meadowlands, NJ. Sweet!

If I figure out the cost and the logistics it can't be that expensive. Every year the face value of the tickets increases so I factor that in. The teams playing are the Denver Broncos and the Seattle Seahawks. Denver's been in a bunch of Super bowls and Seattle would have to travel across the country to freeze their ass off to see the game. It was a Hometown game for us. No expensive airline tickets or 3-day lodging. No rental cars or meals. This may be one of the least expensive games I ever attended. This was the first cold weather Super Bowl. I didn't think there would be too many fans that want to brave the Northeast winter to sit outside and root for two teams they weren't attached to.

I called Mario, let's go to the game. He says I'm nuts. Mario hates the cold! I go over my thought process that this would be a hassle-free game to get to and he agrees. We decide to make it a family event. He would check into securing tickets. I inform him that I'm taking my son and I'll purchase my own tickets. He was extremely generous with the previous year's game. He informs his wife and we all plan a tailgate. The stage is set there would be 13 of us in all and we would meet at a predetermined spot and drive in together as security would be tight. The SUV's were stocked with everything from pulled pork, expresso machines, Johnny Walker Blue and hand warmers. His other friend George secured tickets and he would drive the other SUV.

Being season ticket holders, they knew the heads of security. We were escorted past the massive security and the Guardsman and swat teams carrying M-16's and Uzis. We parked in the same area we usually do prior to Jet Games. It was if we were at a Hometown Game. All the close parking lots were closed. There was a row of about 20 cars besides us. We had the whole place to ourselves. Over the years, I've come to the realize that's how Mario and George roll. Every detail for the celebration is perfect thanks to their wives Lou and Sharon. I'm fortunate to have such generous friends. No one else could have pulled this off!

If our good fortune wasn't enough, we received a break in the weather as a winter storm had stalled over Indiana. It had warmed to the low 40's. I had bought my son a Carhart suit the one-piece outerwear that you see construction workers wear during the winter. We were toasty. We ate the pulled pork that Mario's wife Sharon had prepared and drank from a fully stocked bar. It was two hours before Game time we kept occupied watching the pre-game on a 40-inch TV that rose up from Mario's custom-built Escalade. We threw around the pigskin and played corn hole. It doesn't get much better than this as a football fan.

Chapter 25 Father and Son Reunion

Gameday February 2, 2014. It had been 44 years since my father took me to my first Professional Football game at Shea stadium that cold crisp late Fall day. Now I would be taking my 14-year-old son into Giants Stadium to see his first Super Bowl. I had promised to take him once the Jets finally won enough games to get in. Unfortunately, that hasn't transpired. I was 53 years old now and I decided it was time to share this experience with him. So, there we were walking into the stadium together. My first Super Bowl was in 1991 with my younger brother. Now 23 years later I would be sharing this experience with my teenage son.

Most pre-game activities were offsite due to weather concerns. There were a limited amount of concessions and places to take pictures with a version of the Lombardi Trophy and player cut outs. We had the one ticket that counted and 90 minutes prior to kickoff we were on line to enter the stadium. My friend had VIP tickets and all thirteen of us entered through his gate. It took about 25 minutes to pass the final checkpoint. The weather was about 48 degrees we dodged a bullet that day as the following Monday there was a blizzard in the Northeast. Only six hours after the game was over the area was blanketed by 8 inches of snow. God must really like Football! We entered our gate and we see a sea of green and black Seahawk jerseys with clusters of orange for the Denver Broncos. Our seats were on the 5-yard line in the corner of the Northeast endzone. We were about 40 rows up and surrounded by Seattle fans.

This was second attempt at winning the Super Bowl and the fans were hungry for a championship. The returning champion Broncos were favored by 2 points. Both teams entered the arena at 13-3. It was 5-time NFL MVP Peyton Manning against the upstart Russel Wilson. Ironically this was the Jersey I bought for steve at Big Shots back in October of 2013. The halftime show was Bruno Mars and the Red Hot Chili Peppers. Joe Buck and Troy Aikman broadcasted the game for Fox. Renee Fleming sang the National Anthem. The Military Jets fly over, and the game begins.

Seattle kicks off and Denver has the ball on the 14-yard line. The very first play from scrimmage Peyton Manning and Center Manny Ramirez have a botched snap which leads to a Seahawk's safety. The first play and it's 2-0. It was all downhill from there. The Seahawks dominated every facet of the game. By the time the final whistle blew it was Seahawks 42 and Denver 3. It was supposed to be the number one Offense Denver against the "Legion of Doom" best ranked Defense Seattle Seahawks. It was the first time an underdog team won by such a large margin. We might as well have just gone to a Bruno Mars concert, it would have been a hell of a lot cheaper. Never did the cliché "Defense wins Championships" ring truer. Either way my son enjoyed the experience. It's something he will cherish for a long time. Our kids grow up so fast, anytime we get to spend this much time with them or experience something new jump at the opportunity.

I guess I was due for a blowout after attending all those last-minute finishes. Financially, it would have been worse if we had to fly and pay for hotels and meals. It's just amazing that the line on the game was so wrong. A 2-point favorite loses by 35 points. It had to be the largest disparity in Super Bowl history.

Below are Pictures of 13 of us tailgating in the empty parking lot at Met Life Stadium four hours prior to kickoff

Baker's Dozen!

The gang of 13 (Myself and son, Roger and his sister, Mario & George and their families and Marco and his son) that attended the first Cold Weather Super Bowl in history at Met Life Stadium!

Chapter 26 Friday Night Lights

In Football Stadiums across America fans gather to watch the local High School kids play Football on Friday Nights. You can hear the drums of the HS Band, the ref's whistles and the cheering fans as you walk from the parking lot to the bleachers. The excitement of cross-town rivals is passed down through generations. The game has changed since I played it's faster and the plays are more complex. But the Spirit and love for this game remains the same. To be successful you must dedicate yourself to long days of hard work and sacrifice.

Ever since I began writing over the Summer, I wondered how I would end this book. I received the answer on October 6th, 2018.

This book has spanned 48 years, almost a lifetime of playing and watching this Great American sport of Football. It started in 1970 when I attended my first NY Jets game in Shea Stadium with my Dad and two brothers. It ends on October 6th on a night game at my Alma Mater Monsignor Farrell High School in Oakwood, Staten Island.

In late August, I received an email from a former teammate. The School planned to honor our 1978 undefeated team at halftime under the lights. It had been 40 years since our nationally ranked team had run the table at a perfect 9-0. When I entered Freshman year we had 300 boys in our class. By the time we graduated we were 288. Our Football team the Monsignor Farrell Lions were comprised of 54 Junior and Senior players. On October 6th 34 players showed up to walk onto the new astro-turf field under the bright lights to be honored.

On the drive to Staten Island from the Jersey Shore I reflected on all the hard work it took to achieve that goal so long ago. In the Summer, we would gather for two hours every night at Marine Park and workout, run and condition for six weeks. Then if you made the team you were off to camp in the aptly named town of Pittsfield, Massachusetts. We lived in rustic cabins ate crappy food and practiced 3 times a day. It was a Spartan existence at best. Sacrificing the last weeks of Summer while others were laying on the beach. Once School started and we had to juggle heavy work-loads of home work along with 2 to 3 hours of practice every night. We didn't have any lights on the field but that never seemed to matter as we practiced until we couldn't see the ball. We never complained we just trudged through it. In the off season, we lifted weights three times a week from January to May. It was a full-time job. The final result? We were quicker, stronger and more prepared then our opponents. Over the three years that I played we lost 3 games. In the Fall of 1978 we didn't lose any! A perfect 9 and 0!

To be honest with you, I had all but forgotten about this achievement. After all it had been 40 years and life goes on. When people talked about their experiences or "Glory Days" I rarely joined in unless they pressed. When pressed I would tell them we were ranked number 13 in the country. That as Juniors we had chartered a jet and played the number one team in the nation Moeller High School in Cincinnati. That it was written up in Sports Illustrated as the Super Bowl of High School football. That our Quarterback "Ziggy" received a full scholarship to Notre Dame and our Center Tony had a full ride to Boston University. That we had the best team in NYC and State that year. Then I'd say that & a quarter will get you on the bus! I was always in the camp that you enjoy your success but live in the present and don't dwell on the past. There were many more accomplishments to achieve in the future. Always move forward, work hard and be humble.

They say you can never go home again. But on October 6th, 2018 we did. I would have never even thought about the 40th year anniversary. After all we didn't celebrate the 10th or 25th. But here I was in the car with my girlfriend Jenny driving back through time. Jenny was a Jersey Girl who was curious to see where I had grown up. It was 1979, since I had last seen most of my teammates. I walked into La Fontana Restaurant across from the school at 5:30 where we had planned to gather. No one shook hands we all hugged each other. We walked across to the field and took several group pictures. We watched the game from the senior balcony.

The group was comprised of 3 Lawyers, Doctors, Dentists and Engineers. There were 10 Wall Street Investment Bankers and Brokers. My teammate Tony and I had worked at Goldman Sachs. There were several successful business owners. There were a couple of Cops and Fireman who had retired and had successful second careers. There were 2 Grandfathers while 3 others were already retired! The common theme was everyone had continued working hard after graduation. Over the years a couple of guys had died. But out of 55 players 34 had made the concerted effort to be there together. The hard work academically and the sacrifice & dedication on the gridiron carried over into our professional careers. The Christian Brothers, Teachers and Coaches at Monsignor Farrell High School prepared us for life. Our parents sacrificed and took on the financial burden to send that. In 1975, we entered as boys in 1979 we left as men! We were well prepared to tackle college and to face what life deals you. *Vir Fidelis!* The faithful men!

At halftime, our captains and my JV coach Mike Marino led us out to the field. Coach Marino taught me how to play my positions. He was the best damn coach I ever had. Unfortunately our Head Coach, the Legendary Dennis Barrett was under the weather and was unable to attend. We walked onto the field as they read our names. Players traveled from Florida, California, South Carolina and Chicago. Others drove in from Massachusetts, Upstate NY and Pennsylvania. It had been 34 years since I last saw my youngest brother play at Farrell. It was so surreal! It felt as if we were kids again. It felt like time had stopped as the crowd cheered, and we received a standing ovation. We had spent so much time together as a group but that was 40 years ago. Yet here we were one of the three undefeated teams in the school's 60-year history.

Football is a game of controlled chaos. It's a highly competitive sport that forces 11 guys to act as one team focused on achieving one goal together. You play this game because you love it. It rewards you as it teaches life lessons. In the end, as you walk off the field for the last time you are left with whatever is up on the scoreboard. All along the way there's this intangible feeling of comradery that's difficult to explain. If you're as fortunate as the '78 Lions, you will have lifetime loyal friends.

Back on the balcony we watched the end of the game and talked about our life experiences. Many of us had children that were either in College or had already finished. My cousins and their kids showed up and we took pictures with the field in the background.

After the game we drove to the town Eltingville to gather at Joe O'Toole's Joyce's Tavern. He was a Junior on our team. I stayed for about an hour telling old stories and discussing what had transpired in our lives. Ken a lawyer who lives in Connecticut, was talking to another player whose son goes to school at Fairfield. He gave him his number and said if he ever wants a home cooked meal or needs a break his son was always welcome at his house.

I went to St Clare's and Farrell with Mike Noone and Steve Gilmartin. We've known each other for 50 years! Rendy built a lakeside house upstate extended an invitation to come up for a week and stay. This is the way it always was. You see, it didn't matter what car you drove what house you lived in. That doesn't define who you are as an individual. We were and still are a family. If it wasn't for the common thread of Football, we would not have had such close-knit relationships. I thanked Fitzy for setting this up. I never would have thought of all us getting honored like that. It was a special night that I'll remember for a long time. I hugged my teammates and said goodbyes. On the drive home, I shared more stories with Jenny. She commented on what a great group of guys we were. I was so happy to see all the guys! It wasn't until I hit the sack that night that I realized that would probably be the last time we would all be together in one place. I realized how lucky I was to have experienced that chapter of my life. What a special time and place to grow up in. I wish everyone could experience that opportunity.

Below is a picture of the 1978 Undefeated Farrell Lions!

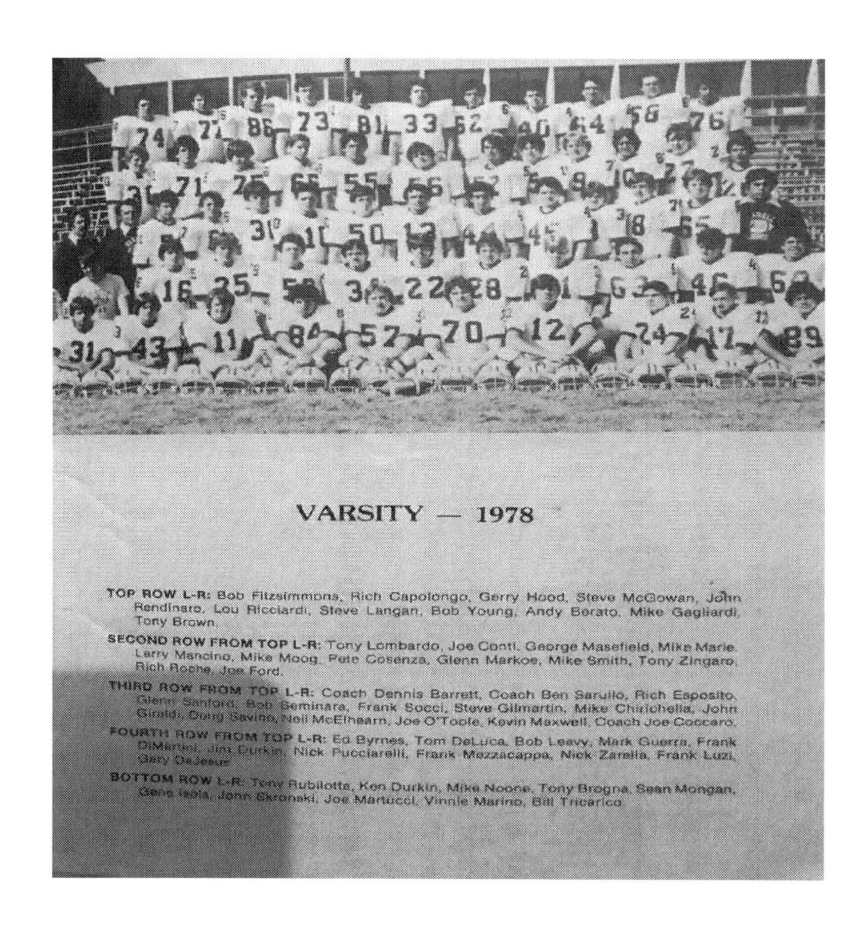

Rendy and I at the 40th Reunion ready to be honored on the Field at halftime

The two Offensive Guards Stephen Gilmartin and myself. We were also College roommates

Chapter 27 The Circle Goes Round

On October 13, 2018 Mario calls me and invites me to the Jet game on Sunday the 14th. I say sure why not. It's a nice Fall day. He instructs me to meet him in Lyndhurst at 9:30 AM for a 1 o'clock game. I usually roll into these games 90 minutes before kickoff. My buddy Mario wants to get there early set up tailgate and have fun. So, what the hell I'll get up there a couple of hours earlier. He and his buddy George have the best seats in the house. Right on the 50-yard line!

These guys are professional tailgaters. Cuban cigars, excellent scotch & wine. A Bose Stereo set up that would make a DJ jealous. Pop the Escalade's tailgate and you have a 40-inch TV inside and even an expresso maker! I always appreciate their generosity. A few days earlier I thought I heard they were honoring Joe Namath and the 1969 Champion Jets. At halftime they would be on the field. I ran into another friend whose buddy had a special bracelet to get on the field. We enter the stadium they hand us towels with the 1969 Jets autographs! This book spans over 49 years of my life. It began in 1970 watching the NY Jets at Shea Stadium. I attempted to get Joe Namath's Autograph when I was 9 years old. Now it culminates with me getting the whole teams autograph as I enter the Met Life Stadium! Could this be another opportunity to get his autograph or even meet him 48 years later?

Now this is the final chapter of the book. At this point in the book, one could make the case that I'm pretty resourceful. Come Hell or Highwater I am getting on that damn field! There was 5 minutes until halftime. I had to think quick. Mario's seats are Club Box seats. They are entitled to the private lounge where food and offer bar services are included. It's a private lounge that opens right up to the field behind the visiting team's bench. Once they scan your ticket they give you a colored wrist band. I leave my seat and enter the lounge. I see my buddy and ask if they are going on the field. He informs me they already left. I tell them I'm getting on that field no matter what. Take pictures when I'm out there.

I jog through the bowels of Giants stadium feverishly scanning for the entrance to the field. I could hear the broadcaster announce the half time score. Fans are exiting their seats in a frantic search for the restrooms. The hall is more crowded. I cut right, then left like OJ through the airport, avoiding the patrons. Then I hit a dead end a solid wall. Suddenly, a door swings open. I spy about 40 people gathered in the tunnel forming an orderly line to enter the field. I have one shot to get in. There's an usher at the door. I hold up my arm with the wrist band as I jog past. Now I see there's about 100 people already lined up to walk onto the field. I go around the back of the line and work my way up into the center. Security is everywhere. If they attempt to weed me out it will be a tougher task. I position myself right in the middle as we start to walk onto the field. I blend in perfectly. My objective is to get a picture with Joe Namath. He is positioned on the Jet's logo at midfield. I'm 30 yards away on the left hashmark. He starts to talk, and I try to get closer.

I'm on the 25-yd line now. I see my buddy's in the lower lounge. They snap some pics of me as they laugh in disbelief !!!. In 1970, Joe Namath refused to sign my autograph as a kid. Now I have a second chance. I will not be denied! I'm on the 30-yard line. He stops talking and the crowd cheers. I realize my time is waning

I cross the 35. Now the security starts to herd us back towards the tunnel. I'm going against the grain. I'm like a salmon swimming up-stream. Security personnel make a human chain. They are carrying a yellow rope and they are walking towards me. One last push, I see Joe walking off toward the Jets sideline. He is on the 45. I yell Joe Willy! But to no avail. Security beckons "Clear the Field"! Two guards in yellow wind breakers are quickly approaching. It was 4th and goal! My last chance! Suddenly... Deja Vue! A desperate analogy popped into my head. It was a flashback to former Jet coach Joe Walton. He called a screen play on 4th and long. Just like he did when he was coach. The whole stadium gasped in disbelief. Deja Vue! What a nightmare. It was the wrong play and I would be tackled for a loss! Sure enough, I was stopped dead at the 38-yard line 7 yards short! Joe vanishes into the crowd.

Go Jets!!!   J- E- T- S   JETS JETS JETS!!!

Pic Below: I am on the field at Met Life Stadium halftime at the Jets Game October 14th

The Author at a Book Signing

37885629R00117

Made in the USA
Columbia, SC
02 December 2018